FELONY REVIEW

FELONY REVIEW

TALES OF TRUE CRIME AND CORRUPTION IN CHICAGO

∵

RANDY E. BARNETT

© 2026 by Randy E. Barnett

All Rights Reserved.
No part of this publication may be reproduced,
stored in a retrieval system, or transmitted, in any form or by
any means, electronic, mechanical, photocopying, recording,
or otherwise, without the prior written permission of
Encounter Books, 900 Broadway, Suite 601,
New York, New York 10003.

First American edition published in 2026 by Encounter Books,
an activity of Encounter for Culture and Education, Inc.,
a nonprofit, tax exempt corporation.
Encounter Books website address: www.encounterbooks.com

Manufactured in Canada and printed on acid-free paper.
The paper used in this publication meets the minimum requirements of
ANSI/NISO Z39.48–1992 (R 2009) (*Permanence of Paper*).

LIBRARY OF CONGRESS CATALOGING-IN-PUBLICATION DATA
Information for this title can be found at the Library of Congress
website under the following ISBN 978-1-64177-495-6.

To Judges John Crowley and Eugene Pincham,
and my fellow Cook County State's Attorneys,
from whom I learned so much.

FOREWORD

RANDY BARNETT IS truly a contemporary man for all seasons. I first encountered his mind when he was my student at Harvard Law School. In a class filled with brilliant students, many of them knee-jerk liberals, Randy stood out as a principled legal analyst who did not allow partisanship to influence his reading of the Constitution, statutes, or other sources of the law. He was a breath of fresh air who challenged me with brilliant defenses of his somewhat out-of-fashion opinions.

Not content to limit his experience to academia, Randy became a prosecutor in one of the most crime-ridden cities in the country. What he learned in the police stations and courtrooms of Chicago he now conveys in this entertaining account that reads like a television reality series.

But Randy would make his career neither in the courtroom nor on the street, but rather in the classroom and the library, where his path-breaking books on originalism and the Constitution became the gold standard for judges and professors alike. Today no one can write about constitutional interpretation without referencing the challenging ideas of Randy Barnett.

Randy's ideas are a function not only of his unusual mind, but of his eyes and ears. He well understands the relationship between experience and ideology. He is a great professor because he was a good lawyer. And he was a good lawyer because he always had the mind of a professor.

This book is a joy to read for lawyers and laypeople alike. It tells fascinating stories about deeply flawed human beings on all sides of the criminal justice system: guilty defendants, innocent defendants; excellent prosecutors, not so excellent prosecutors; good defense lawyers, not so good defense lawyers; honest judges, not so honest judges. These are the human realities of our criminal justice system, and Randy brings them to life with his remarkable ability to recall and relate.

Randy's prior books provided a top-down view of the legal system, from Mount Olympus, or at least from the ivory tower. In Felony Review: Tales of True Crime and Corruption in Chicago, he allows us to glimpse the system from the bottom up. It is this combination of perspectives that makes Randy Barnett such a formidable commentator on the criminal justice system.

As a retired professor, and sometimes practicing lawyer, I too have seen all sides of the system. I can attest to the fact that Randy has it right. His descriptions are right on and his prescriptions are thoughtful. Reading his riveting true crime tales will enlighten you on how our criminal justice really works, which, as he says, is "better than TV."

Felony Review is simply a great read from a great lawyer.

—ALAN DERSHOWITZ,
Felix Frankfurter Professor of Law, Emeritus,
HARVARD LAW SCHOOL

INTRODUCTION: BETTER THAN TV

FEBRUARY 24, 1979, was a cold night in Chicago. Four gangbangers—Luis Ruiz, Juan Caballero, Placido "Rico" LaBoy, and Nelson "Popeye" Aviles—were hanging out at a hamburger joint and gang haunt called King Kastle on Chicago's North Side. Three young men—Michael Salcido, seventeen, his brother Arthur, nineteen, and their friend Frank Mussa, sixteen—approached them. The three had driven a hundred miles from a small city southwest of Chicago in search of weed, and this was where that quest had led them.

Michael asked Ruiz if they had any. The gangbangers said no, because they really didn't have any. But Michael and his companions thought maybe the gangbangers just didn't trust them. So he tried to ingratiate himself by asking if the four knew a guy named Jose Cortez. Cortez was a big-shot member of the Latin Eagles, a notorious street gang. Ruiz said, Yeah, he knew Cortez and asked Michael if he was a member of the Latin Eagles. Michael said, Yeah, he was, and so were his brother and friend. But Michael was lying about that; he was a kid from the suburbs and no gang member of any kind. He just wanted to get high and was willing to say anything that he thought might score them a joint or two.

Ruiz said he and his three buddies were also Latin Eagles. That got Michael bragging about having been with Eagles on drive-by hits on other gangsters. He even claimed to have acted as the driver for a hit on some members of the Latin Queens, the female counterparts to the Latin Kings, who were the foremost rivals of the Latin Eagles.

Well, that seemed to do it. Ruiz said, Yeah, sure, they knew where to score some weed, and he'd be glad to show Michael and his friends. He, too, was lying. The Kings had no pot, not to use and not to sell. All seven got into Michael's mother's car, which he'd borrowed, with Michael, Arthur, and Frank in front.

Michael drove out of the parking lot and followed Ruiz's directions into an alley and stopped where he was told to. The four gang members got out of the back and directed Michael to come with them; they'd show him where to score the weed. Michael eagerly got out, and they all began walking—and as soon as they couldn't be seen by Michael's brother and friend in the car, the four set upon Michael, beating him badly.

They were not Latin Eagles, Ruiz now told him. They were Latin Kings, mortal enemies of the Latin Eagles.

The four gangbangers led Michael back to the car with Aviles holding a knife and LaBoy a gun. Seeing Michael beaten so badly frightened his brother and friend as the five climbed in the car, this time with LaBoy behind the wheel and Michael and Ruiz in back.

LaBoy drove into a T-shaped alley and stopped. He and Caballero took Michael and Frank around the corner of the T at gunpoint and ordered them to lie face down in the snow. Ruiz stayed with the car and watched as Aviles stabbed Arthur. LaBoy then brought Frank back to the car, pushed him into the back seat on top of Arthur, and, with the same knife, stabbed him to death. Finally, Caballero brought Michael to the car, pushed him on top of the bodies of his dying friends, and stabbed him to death, too.

Eight days later—March 4, 1979—at 1:45 a.m., I sat with Caballero, taking his confession, in an interrogation room at the Chicago Police Department's Area 6 Homicide Unit Headquarters, located at Belmont and Western Avenue. What occurred to me as we sat down was how grimly ironic it was that we were at the former site of the old Riverview Park I remembered visiting as a boy from Calumet City. The amusement park's marketing slogan, "Laugh Your Troubles Away," was vivid in my mind.

The other persons in the room with us were Investigator Lee Epplin of the Area 6 Homicide-Sex Unit and Michael Hartnett, a court reporter who worked for the Cook County State's Attorney's Office. It was Hartnett's job to take down every word Caballero said and every question I asked as an assistant state's attorney assigned to the Felony Review Unit of the Cook County State's Attorney's Office.

Under Cook County's innovative Felony Review system, the Chicago Police Department (CPD) could file no felony charges without the approval of an assistant state's attorney (ASA). To make this system function, the State's Attorney created a specialized unit of prosecutors who were stationed in the six Chicago Police Department Area Headquarters then located throughout the city. (In 2012, the Area 6 Headquarters at Belmont and Western was closed as a cost-cutting measure. The number of detective areas was reduced from six to three in 2013, then increased to five in 2020.)

Young prosecutors assigned to Felony Review worked twelve-hour shifts, either 6 a.m. to 6 p.m. or 6 p.m. to 6 a.m.—three days on, three days off. They had their own Chevy Nova squad cars, complete with police radios, that they would use to travel to district police stations or to crime scenes. ASAs graduated to Felony Review after prosecuting misdemeanor cases in the Municipal Division of the Circuit Court of Cook County and were on their way to being felony court prosecutors.

A Felony Review ASA's job was to assess the evidence, interview the cops and the witnesses, conduct lineups, approve search warrants, and obtain statements from the accused, if possible. Many of these statements were either full confessions or otherwise "inculpatory"—which is to say, they would be incriminating down the line. Felony Review meant genuine, authentic review. No rubber-stamping just because the cops had arrested someone. The unit rejected about 40 percent of the cases the CPD called it in to evaluate. My supervisors monitored my rejection rate on a weekly basis.

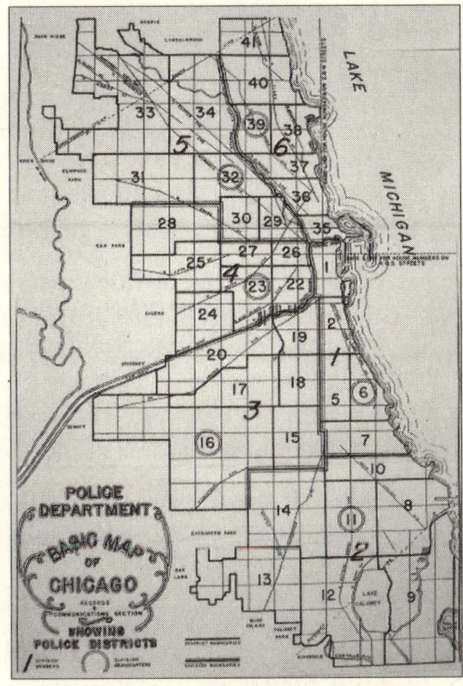

Figure 1. The Six Chicago Police Department Areas, designated by numbers in italics
(courtesy of the Chicago Police Department)

The details of how eighteen-year-old Juan Caballero had murdered Michael Salcido, which he related to me in his court-reported statement, chilled me from head to toe, viscera to epidermis.

> "I told him to close his eyes . . ."
> "You told who to close his eyes?"

"Michael. Michael to close his eyes. I opened up the back door, and I said, 'Close your eyes and lay down,' and he saw him as he was going in, so I had to push him."

"When you say he saw the other guy, what did he do?"

"He didn't say nothing. I guess he must really have freaked."

"Then what happened after you pushed him down?"

"I proceeded to pull back his head and sliced his throat."

"What else did you do?"

"I stabbed him. When I sliced his throat while he was like this, he turned around, I started stabbing him around this area."

"This area meaning . . ."

"Right here."

"The chest."

"The chest area and, you know, his ribs around there."

"Did he turn over after you pushed him in the car?"

"Sort of on his side a little bit, that's when I got him like that. I had to like hook my arm to get him."

"To get him?"

"To get the knife to his chest."

"And then what happened next?"

"Well, I stepped out of the car and I said, you know, 'He is going to die, he is not dead yet.' They said, 'Make sure,' and I went back and stabbed him a couple of more times. I got out of the car then."

"Why did you get out of the car?"

"The guy was going to die and I knew it. I got out of there as fast as I could."

"How many times did you stab him?"

"I don't remember, quite a few times."

"More than ten?"

"Yeah."

"More than twenty?"

"I'd say more than ten at least. Maybe fifteen, ten or fifteen, but not twenty. Then Rico grabbed the knife to make sure he was dead, and he stabbed him some more."

"Do you remember Michael saying anything during that time?"

"Yeah, when I was— After I got out and then he told me to make sure he was dead, I went and stabbed him some more, and [Michael] said, he hollered, 'I'm dead, I'm dead.'"

Juan Caballero and Luis Ruiz were charged with murder on the basis of their confessions. LaBoy and Aviles, who both refused to talk with me, would eventually be charged later.

The *Chicago Sun-Times* reported that "Two men identified by police as members of the Latin Kings street gang were charged with murder Sunday in the slaying of three young men who were found stabbed to death Feb. 25 in a car parked behind 1460 W. Pensacola. Belmont Area homicide investigators, who arrested the men Sunday as a result of tips from informants, said the killings were gang-related." The paper added, "The slaying victims were Michael Salcido; 17, his brother, Arthur, 19, and their friend Frank Mussa, 16, of Princeton, Ill. The Salcido brothers were wards of the state. Michael lived in the Maryville Academy, 1150 N. River Road, Des Plaines, and Arthur lived with a foster family in Princeton."

The *Chicago Tribune* story added an interesting detail: Luis Ruiz had been acquitted of previous murder. When I explained to him the procedure for giving a statement, he told me he'd confessed to a previous murder charge—which he beat—so he knew the procedures. The judge who had acquitted him after a bench trial was Judge Eugene Pincham, who will make a prominent appearance in this book.

4 Section 3 Chicago Tribune, Tuesday, March 6, 1979

Accused killer of 3 freed in prior case

By Jane Fritsch

A 19-YEAR-old street gang member who is charged with slitting the throats of three youths last month had been freed on a murder charge in November by a Circuit Court judge, court records show.

The November action, by Judge R. Eugene Pincham, was denounced as "outrageous and unprecedented" by Michael Angarola, an assistant state's attorney.

Louis Ruiz, of 1445 W. Warner Av., the youth set free by Pincham, is one of three Latin King gang members charged with the slayings of three teenagers whose bodies were found Feb. 24 in a North Side alley.

"He should be in the penitentiary right now," Angarola said of Ruiz.

RECORDS SHOW that in November Ruiz was tried in a bench trial before Pincham for the 1976 murder of Thomas Griebell, 16, of 1540 W. George St.

Ruiz, testifying in his own behalf, admitted from the witness stand that he fired the shot that killed Griebell but insisted that he intended only to fire a warning shot over Griebell's head.

After all the evidence was presented, Pincham, acting on a motion by Ruiz's lawyer, dismissed the murder indictment and allowed Ruiz to go free.

The judge said the indictment was "unfair" because a 16-year-old youth arrested with Ruiz on charges of murdering Griebell had been tried in the juvenile court system and allowed to plead guilty to the lesser charge of involuntary manslaughter.

An appeal filed by the state's attorney's office against Pincham's ruling is pending. Pincham denied a request from Angarola to keep Ruiz in custody until the ruling on the appeal is issued.

RUIZ; LOUIS Caballero, 19, of 2024 N. Whipple St.; and Placido LaBoy, 18, of 4306 N. Clark St., are charged with murdering Michael Salcido, 17, a ward of the state who lived in Maryville Academy in Des Plaines; his brother, Arthur, 19, of Princeton, Ill.; and Frank Musa, 16, son of a Princeton grocer. Ruiz and Caballero were arrested Sunday, LaBoy on Monday. All are in custody.

Police said the victims were knifed to death one at a time after being taken to an alley behind 1460 W. Pensacola Av. The youths had met earlier with Ruiz, Caballero, and LaBoy in an attempt to buy marijuana, according to police, who said the victims apparently mistook the three for members of the Latin Eagles gang and made disparaging remarks about the Latin Kings.

Anarola said that Ruiz had an extensive juvenile crime record before his arrest in 1976 for the Griebell murder. While free on bond and awaiting trial for the Griebell killing he was arrested and convicted for burglary.

Between the time he was set free in November and his arrest on murder charges Sunday he was charged with battery in connection with a traffic dispute, Angarola said.

Last Oct. 26, LaBoy was acquitted by a jury of fatally beating a North Side man in what police described as a robbery attempt.

Figure 2. *Chicago Tribune* story announcing murder charges against Luis Ruiz and Juan Caballero *(courtesy of Chicago Tribune)*

* * *

Fast-forward a year or so.

The case was scheduled to go to trial in front of Judge James Bailey, a judge whose specialty was heater cases—a heater case being a highly publicized case that attracts lots of media attention. You know, heat. If this hadn't been a death-penalty case, Caballero would've probably pled guilty for whatever he could get, knowing that his confession and the rest of the evidence guaranteed that a jury would vote to convict. The only question was whether the jurors would also vote to end his life. It was worth it to him to roll the dice on a jury trial. He was now nineteen years old, and the grievousness of what he'd done meant he would never be a free man and might never live to see thirty, though following the Supreme Court's reinstatement of the death penalty in the 1976 decision *Gregg v. Georgia*, executions were still rare in Illinois. The first execution (which was by lethal injection) in Illinois wouldn't come until 1990. Still, death row is an awful place to spend sixty or seventy years.

Days before trial was to begin, administrators in the Cook County Jail called the State's Attorney's Office, wanting to set up a meeting with the prosecutors. For whatever reason—I didn't yet know why—they invited me along. By now I was a felony trial assistant at the Criminal Court Building located at 26th and California—referred to as "26th and Cal"—and no longer on Felony Review. But I wasn't one of the prosecutors on this case because I would be called to testify during the trial as a witness to the confession.

The meeting took place in the conference room of Judge Bailey's courtroom. What we heard from the jailers was startling. Inside any jail, there are, of course, snitches, and the snitches had picked up information that the Latin Kings were pissed and had put out a hit on the prosecutors. "No Latin King is going to get the death penalty" was what the jail administrators reported they were saying.

On our way out of the meeting, I looked at the two prosecutors, Rich Trainor and Michael Kane, to take their temperature. They didn't seem particularly phased. For that matter, neither was I. Which surprised me. I even joked that since I was not technically one of the prosecutors, maybe I could get a "declaratory judgment" from the Latin Kings as to whether I was on the hit list.

In hindsight, perhaps it we should have taken the threat more seriously than we did. In October 2025, ABC News reported that the Northern District U.S. Attorney's Office, had charged 37-year-old Juan Espinosa-Martinez, an illegal immigrant and ranking member of the Latin Kings, with offering a $10,000 bounty on U.S. Border Patrol Chief Gregory Bovino. Bovino was highly visible during operations in Los Angeles and Chicago. According to the New York Times, Martinez, whose street name was "Monkey," had sent a Snapchat message and an offer for $2000 for information on that official or "10k if u take him down." The Snapchat post included a picture of Bovino and the letters "LK" designating the Latin Kings. This "hit" order was no joke. And, all joking aside, I did not take the threat against us lightly either.

I went back to my office in the high-rise connected to the old courthouse and began wondering what, if anything, I should do with the information. My first thought was about how I actually lived in gang territory. Bittersweet Place, off North Lake Shore Drive in the southern-most edge of the Uptown neighborhood, was Latin Eagles—not Latin Kings—turf. But Kings territory was not far away.

My next thought was that I had a listed phone number. If you checked the phone book or called 411 for Randy Barnett, you'd get both my number and address. Strange as it might seem—given how many Randys there are and how many Barnetts there are—at the time, I was the only Randy Barnett in Chicago. True, I might've been able to get "Information" (a.k.a. 411) to no longer give out the number and address, but there was no way to delete myself from the physical phone book. (Ah, phone books, those artifacts of another era. I think fondly of Steve Martin squealing with glee when the new phone books arrived in *The Jerk* . . . because his name was in it.)

Suppose I was walking home to my apartment building, having parked the car on the street, and a car drove past me with its occupants opening fire. I'd prosecuted drive-by gang shootings, so this was easy to suppose.

My final thought was: *How stupid would I feel if I had been warned but had done nothing to prepare myself for such an eventuality?* Call it the "regret principle." Project yourself into the future and ask your future self how much you would regret having acted a certain way or having failed to act a certain way. I've made many decisions applying that thought experiment, including whether to propose marriage to my wife.

So I opened my right-hand desk drawer in the state's attorney's office and looked at all the handguns I kept there. Each had been used in the commission of crimes I had prosecuted in that courtroom and offered as evidence during trial. Technically, I was required to have them destroyed after the cases were terminated. But for whatever reason, I couldn't bring myself to do that. I removed a few from the drawer and examined them. Most were cheap, but a few were pretty decent weapons. The easiest thing to do would be to, ahem, "borrow" one for a while, just in case.

But that would also be the dumbest thing to do, as it would've put my professional future, as opposed to my life, in jeopardy. My life in jeopardy was only theoretical. My career in jeopardy was in no way theoretical if I'd been caught taking one of those guns.

You see, it wasn't legal for a state's attorney to carry a gun. If I were caught in possession of *any* firearm, I would be in trouble, though under the circumstances the bosses would likely understand and forgive the transgression after administering a metaphorical hand slap. But if I were caught in possession of a gun that had a Chicago Police Department Crime Lab number etched into its side? A number that connected it to a criminal shooting? Katie, bar the jail door. That kind of stupidity could not be forgiven, either by the bosses or the state bar.

And so I decided that the least-bad course of action was to borrow my dad's Smith & Wesson .38 Special revolver. He had purchased the gun in 1967 after receiving numerous threats from disgruntled customers of his full-service laundry located on 71st Street on the South Side of Chicago. Tough as he was, after a while, he just could not face the prospect of working in his store and walking to his car after dark without carrying a pistol in his front pocket for protection. He

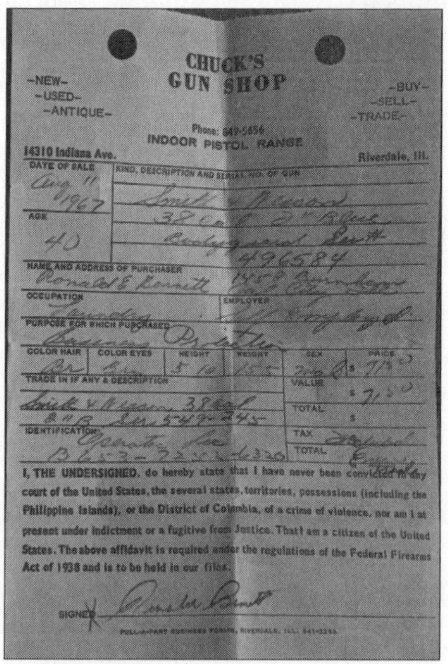

CHUCK'S
GUN SHOP

-NEW- -USED- -ANTIQUE-

-BUY- -SELL- -TRADE-

Phone: 849-5656
INDOOR PISTOL RANGE

14310 Indiana Ave. Riverdale, Ill.

DATE OF SALE: Aug 11 1967
KIND, DESCRIPTION AND SERIAL NO. OF GUN: 496584
AGE: 40
NAME AND ADDRESS OF PURCHASER:
OCCUPATION:
EMPLOYER:
PURPOSE FOR WHICH PURCHASED:
COLOR HAIR: | COLOR EYES: | HEIGHT: 5 10 | WEIGHT: | SEX: | PRICE: $
TRADE IN IF ANY & DESCRIPTION:
VALUE: $
TOTAL: $
IDENTIFICATION:
TAX:
TOTAL:

I, THE UNDERSIGNED, do hereby state that I have never been convicted in any court of the United States, the several states, territories, possessions (including the Philippine Islands), or the District of Columbia, of a crime of violence, nor am I at present under indictment or a fugitive from Justice. That I am a citizen of the United States. The above affidavit is required under the regulations of the Federal Firearms Act of 1938 and is to be held in our files.

SIGNED

Figure 3. Receipt for Smith & Wesson revolver
(courtesy of Howard Barnett)

bought the gun for $71.50 from Chuck's Gun Shop. Such a vintage gun would sell today for $400–500. Under "purpose for which purchased," the sales receipt says, "business protection."

In 1967, I was fifteen years old, and I sometimes worked at his store loading and unloading washing machines and dryers and waiting on customers. At my dad's insistence, I'd learned to shoot the gun in case he was ever overpowered or disabled by an attacker and I had to defend myself. His J-frame Model 49 Bodyguard carried five rounds and featured a hammer shroud so it would not catch on your pants as you drew it from your pocket. This model still makes a perfectly handy pocket pistol for self-defense.

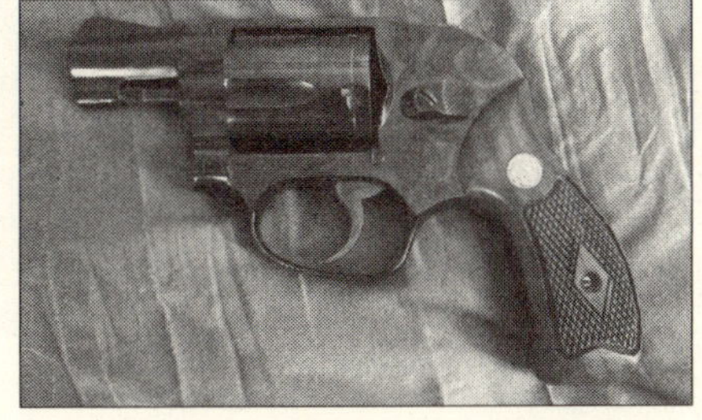

Figure 4. Ronald Barnett's Smith & Wesson Model 49 Bodyguard *(courtesy of Howard Barnett)*

I drove out to my parents' home in the southwest suburb of Orland Park to pick it up. I told my dad why I was borrowing it, but not my mom. (I'm sure you understand.)

I couldn't remember the last time I'd fired a gun, so the next stop was a gun range. Perhaps I went to Chuck's Gun Shop, which had an indoor pistol range and was just a thirty-minute drive from my parents' home. My brother Howard recalls that when I got to the range, they turned me away on account of all the lanes being occupied. So I did what any self-respecting state's attorney would do. I showed them my state's attorney's ID, which in Cook County had the power of Aladdin's genie, and told them I really needed to practice.

Two minutes later, they miraculously found a place for me, and I ran several cylinders through before cleaning the gun, loading it up again, and putting it in my

State's Attorney's Office
County of Cook - State of Illinois
This will certify that:
Randy E. Barnett
is a duly appointed Assistant State's Attorney for all purposes of representing the State of Illinois, in such capacity, in the County of Cook. He/She is also authorized to perform such other functions as directed by the State's Attorney, County of Cook, State of Illinois.
RICHARD M. DALEY, State's Attorney
SIGNATURE
D.O.B. 2/5/52
HGT. 5'11"
WGT. 160
EYES Brown
HAIR Brown
RIGHT INDEX

Figure 5. State's Attorney's Office identification card

briefcase. Those short-barreled revolvers were made for close combat, not distance, but it still felt comforting to have the thing with me.

In those days, people entering the Criminal Court Building had to pass through metal detectors, but lawyers got to bypass them. For several weeks, until the trial was far in the rearview mirror, with Caballero convicted on all counts and sentenced to death, I carried that gun in my briefcase.

This was not TV. This was real life.

PART I: PAYING MY DUES

From Cal City to the Cook County State's Attorney's Office

IN A LIFE *for Liberty: The Making of an American Originalist*, I describe the circuitous route I took from Calumet City, Illinois, to helping to restore our lost Constitution by developing the theory of originalism, and then helping to get Supreme Court justices selected who would be inclined to adopt this approach. None of that was according to some grand plan. Way back when, beginning at age nine, I'd intended to become a criminal trial lawyer, thanks to the TV series *The Defenders*, starring E.G. Marshall and Robert Reed as the father-son criminal defense firm of Preston & Preston in Manhattan.

The Defenders was filmed on location in New York City and presented the practical and ethical challenges of being a criminal defense lawyer. In the series, the prosecutors and judges were all depicted as honorable men, sometimes collaborating with the Prestons to see that justice was done. I later came to realize that *The Defenders* resonated with me because, unlike *Perry Mason*, which was about solving murders, this series was about the actual practice of law and was built on the notion of justice. In the early 1960s, just a handful of years after the end of World War II, that notion still seemed as American as Mom and apple pie. At least for me. It doesn't take much self-reflection to see that, if there's been a unifying theme of my life and career, it's the pursuit of justice.

I grew up in Calumet City, Illinois, a town of about 28,000 south of Chicago on the border where Illinois meets northwest Indiana, an area known as "the Region." I used to ride my bike on State Line Road, zigzagging from state to state. Cal City was a Christian town, with four Catholic Churches and a large Polish community; a bedroom community for the white-collar and blue-collar workers who labored in the nearby steel mills and oil refineries of Gary and East Chicago, Indiana.

Very few Jews lived in Cal City. I was one of four in my graduating class of four hundred. The Jewish community was across the state line in Hammond, with the more affluent living in Munster. That's where I attended Temple Beth El, a Reform congregation, where I had my bar mitzvah.

My dad, Ronald Evan Barnett, was a veteran of World War II who served in the US Army Air Corps. He was being trained as a pilot when the war drew to a close, so he didn't get the chance to serve overseas. His father, my grandfather Hiram Barnett, was a US Army ambulance driver in Europe in World War I, an experience that made him an atheist Jew. His father, my great-grandfather Harris Barnett, was a Russian immigrant who changed the family name from Konefsky. He enlisted in the US Army in Chicago a week after "Custer's Last Stand" at the Little Bighorn. On his enlistment form, his occupation was listed as "peddler." He was discharged honorably in the Montana Territory, which means he fought in the Indian wars as an infantryman, before returning to Chicago to raise his family.

My dad wanted to be a lawyer, but his parents wanted him and his brother Robert ("Bobby") to go into the laundry business with their father. Dad took two years of accountancy school instead, so he could do the books for the business. In 1948, my grandfather, my dad, and my uncle founded H. Barnett & Sons. Their first laundry was in the Chatham neighborhood on Cottage Grove Avenue, and they later added a second, larger facility in Chicago's South Shore neighborhood on 71st Street, a half block off Stoney Island Avenue. But just four years later, at age fifty-five, my grandfather dropped dead of a heart attack in front of the store. I was barely a month old.

CITY OF CHICAGO

No 1080 LAUNDRY $[illegible]

BY AUTHORITY OF THE

CITY of CHICAGO

PERMISSION IS HEREBY GIVEN

Name [illegible]

Address [illegible]

CHICAGO, ILL.

1948

to conduct, operate, maintain or carry on the business of a laundry at address stated above, in said City, until the FIRST DAY OF JANUARY NEXT, subject to the ordinances of said City in such case made and provided, and to revocation by the Mayor at any time in his discretion.

Maximum No. of Employes [illegible]

WITNESS the hand of the Mayor of said City, and the Corporate Seal thereof, this 3 day of Aug. 1948.

NOTE—This License Expires December 31, 1948

Martin H Kennelly, Mayor

Attest [illegible], City Clerk

THIS LICENSE MUST BE POSTED IN A CONSPICUOUS PLACE UPON THE LICENSED PREMISES

Figure 6. Business license for my father's laundry business

My dad and his brother worked two jobs. They ran the laundry six days a week and started Barnett Brothers Tune-Up service in Bobby's garage behind his house, where they spent Sundays tuning up cars. Both Dad and his brother bought identical 750-square-foot, two-bedroom, one-bath houses in Calumet City on the same block of heavily trafficked, four-lane Burnham Avenue.

They had chosen Calumet City because the Calumet Expressway, which became I-94 as the interstate highway system was built out, then ended at 159th Street. Cal City was as far as they could get from Chicago and still be able to commute back to their South Side business in a reasonable time. And being farther from the city meant more-affordable homes.

When I was three years old, my nickname for my dad was "most man." He was what you'd call an alpha today. He grew up in the South Shore neighborhood of Chicago, where he ran with a Jewish gang of kids that got into street fights with non-Jews. During one fight, his buddy got thrown through a plate-glass storefront window.

Dad was also the ultimate contrarian. When other Jews were moving from the city to the western or northern suburbs, he moved south, where there were no Jews to speak of. Not being religious, he didn't give this a second thought. He was a Republican Jew, as his father had been. And he was a rock-ribbed conservative Republican in the days when the establishment Republican Party was led by the likes of not-so-conservative Nelson Rockefeller.

I got my political principles from my dad. He believed in justice, and he raised my brother and me in a just fashion. I only lied to my parents one time, when I denied stealing a candy cigarette from my younger brother. My dad went to the store, bought a pack of candy cigarettes, and counted how many there were. Now he had proof that I had lied, and I got my first and last spanking—last because I never needed another one. That ordeal was also, not so incidentally, my first exposure to what you'd have to agree was a prosecution. Dad would have made a superb attorney.

He loved my brother and me but had little use for us until we were old enough to carry on a conversation. At dinner, he would opine at length on current events with positions that always seemed logical and well grounded. Never in doubt, he always had reasons for his views. I tried to emulate him, though by temperament I was more like my mom, who was the court of equity in our home alongside my dad's court of law.

In Calumet City, I was a good student and well-liked by my teachers.

In retrospect, I see that I often got by on "smarts" rather than doing complete due diligence—a character flaw that has persisted ever since. I started playing clarinet in our renowned grade school band, which performed the 1964 New York World's Fair and in Madison Square Garden when I was in the 7th grade. (Eventually, I segued to rhythm guitar and formed a rock band called the Royal Knights.) That same year, I also debated on behalf of Barry Goldwater in front of my entire grade school student body in the school gym. If you recall how badly LBJ beat Goldwater in the '64 election, you'd have to agree that I, too, had no problem being a contrarian.

Cal City was a tough town. I got into my first fight in 2nd grade when I hit a kid on the playground who called me a "dirty Jew." But I grew up in the "nice" part of town, a subdivision of newly built tiny tract homes called "The Gold Coast." In high school, fistfights were commonplace. I did my best to avoid them and was largely successful. But there were a few fights I could not avoid. When that happened, I stood my ground and punched back, inspired by my taciturn but tough father. The instinct he instilled in me would serve me well as a criminal prosecutor, as would growing up with lower- and lower-middle-class kids of the sort I would one day encounter as cops, clerks, and colleagues.

My high school days were spent mostly among other "good" students doing the things good students do. I was president of the student council, served on the high school advisory committee of Democrat Congressman Abner Mikvah, and joined the speech and debate team. I testified at the 1970 Illinois Constitutional Convention *against* lowering the voting age to eighteen.

But I was also on the wrestling team. And as a harbinger of my future career in law enforcement, when a freshman I was designated Calumet City Police Chief for a day.

Even so, my academic aspirations were modest, at best, thanks to my cultural isolation, which was a form of ignorance. My sole aspiration was to attend the University of Illinois until my high school guidance counselor met with me to discuss my SAT test results.

Figure 7. Calumet City Police Chief badge

"With your score, you could get into Northwestern," he said.

"Really?" I replied. "Where's that?"

My best friend and I drove up to Evanston and saw the beauty of Northwestern on Lake Michigan, so now I applied to two colleges—and my counselor had been right. I did get in. Thankfully, Northwestern gave me enough financial aid to make the cost what it would have been at the University of Illinois.

Like my dad, I was pretty much only interested in politics. Because of that I naturally decided to become a political science major at Northwestern. Then I discovered, to my chagrin, that poli-sci was solely about empirical surveys and such, rather than political theory. For reasons I no longer remember, in my second quarter I took an introduction to philosophy class. Back in Cal City, I'd never heard of this thing called "philosophy," and I had no idea there was an actual field of study, the subject of which was justice. This was a revelation. Thanks to the quarter system, I was able to quickly switch my major while still a freshman.

In the spring quarter, I took ethics from Professor Henry B. Veatch, a preeminent natural law philosopher, and ever since, I have been a natural law advocate. Henry treated me like a graduate student, and I took every philosophy course I could, eventually graduating with departmental honors after submitting my thesis "In Defense of Political Anarchism," which was the result of having discovered libertarianism during my junior year. I even flirted with becoming a philosophy professor instead of a lawyer, but ultimately decided to stay the course. I assumed that I'd be enrolling in Northwestern's law school until I got a surprisingly high LSAT score. Suddenly, the holy grail of Harvard Law School (HLS) was now thinkable. I applied and was accepted.

At HLS, my goal was still to become a criminal lawyer, like the father and son in *The Defenders*, and I steadfastly resisted the peer pressure not to "waste" my Harvard law degree. That steadfast resistance was and is needed by anyone at an elite law school not pursuing a judicial clerkship, or a job with Big Law, or both.

Happily for me, Harvard then offered an innovative, intense nine-hour course that combined trial advocacy, ethics, and a clinical component devoted to practicing criminal law in Middlesex County, where Cambridge is located. In that course, I opted for the Harvard Student Prosecutors

Program and prosecuted misdemeanor cases under the close supervision of former Assistant U.S. Attorney Nick Littlefield. I also worked on a Boston murder case while interning for a Suffolk County Assistant District Attorney, and I clerked for the Cook County State's Attorney's Office during the summer between my second and third years of law school and again after graduation.

In all these ways, my law school years actually did prepare me to practice criminal law, and I did become a state court prosecutor in the Cook County State's Attorney's Office in Chicago. The experience was life-changing. As I tell my students, "It was better than TV."

In this book, I will tell the tales of my rise from felony arraignments, to misdemeanor branch courts, to misdemeanor jury courts, to auto theft court, to Felony Review, and finally to the felony trial courts at 26th and California. There I went from a 3rd chair to a 2nd, before ending my tenure as a 1st chair in a felony trial courtroom.

But that was no ordinary time to be a Cook County State's Attorney. The rapid expansion of the criminal courts in response to the crime wave that hit the U.S. in the 1960s and '70s meant I could rise faster than is possible today.

And then there was the corruption, endemic and unavoidable. My career as a criminal prosecutor was not only the story of fighting crime; it was at least as much about working in, but not being tainted by, the Cook County criminal justice system.

I remember those years as a wild ride that offered many lessons that both law students and anyone interested in the law should know.

As for everyone else—well, it really was better than TV.

Becoming a Prosecutor

IN MY SECOND year at Harvard, I interned for Alice Richmond, a Harvard Law grad who was an assistant district attorney in Boston. From my time with her, I learned two valuable lessons. The first came when we were interviewing witnesses for the murder case on which I was assisting. We happened to come upon some exculpatory evidence that had the potential to be helpful to the defense. The law and Supreme Court case law (*Brady v. Maryland*) require prosecutors to disclose such evidence to the defense, though doing so runs up against the competitive instinct to win the case. Alice insisted we had no choice but to disclose the information:

"Every morning," she told me, "I have to look at myself in the mirror."

Ever since, whenever I've been faced with a choice between ethics and seeming self-interest—or just inertia—I hear her voice saying that.

At trial, Alice had me sit with her at the counsel table, which was a great thrill. There I learned a second lesson. During a recess, the bailiff came over to where I was seated, took me aside, and said, "The judge asked me to tell you to turn your chair so your back is to the jury."

Shocked, I asked why.

"Because you are facially reacting to the testimony of the witness, and he does not want the jury to see that."

Wow. I had no idea I was doing that, but I vowed right then that never again would I allow my face to react to whatever might be happening in court. However embarrassing the feedback, it proved to be extraordinarily helpful down the line.

To wit: As a felony trial assistant, when I prepared my witnesses to testify, I had to warn them about the configuration of the courtroom. From where they were seated between the judge's bench to their left and the jury box in front of them, the side of the bench would obstruct their view of the defendant, who was seated to their left at the defense table. So I'd instruct them that, when I asked them to identify their assailant in court, they needed to lean forward and look around the courtroom before making their identification.

Figure 8. View of witness box to the left of the bench

During one bench trial, however, when I asked my witness to tell the court whether she could see her assailant in the courtroom, she didn't remember to lean forward and so couldn't see the defendant. Panicking, she pointed to a police officer who was seated in the spectators' gallery.

Ordinarily, once an identification is made by such a gesture, I would say, "The record will reflect that the witness has identified the defendant," and then state his name as a way of ensuring that it becomes a part of the record. But since she hadn't done that, this time I simply continued my examination without reacting, so neither did defense counsel, who presumably assumed that the identification had been made as usual.

Then, as the witness continued to relate the events that had victimized her, I asked, "Would you lean forward and look around the room and tell us if you see the man who did that in the courtroom?"

To this the defense attorney objected: "Asked and answered."

It's possible he belatedly realized that something was off with the original identification. But the trial judge then said, "She may answer." And this time the witness identified the defendant, and I completed the identification with "The record will reflect . . ."

The other moral of this story is the importance of remaining in the trial judge's good graces.

TV lawyers constantly test the patience of trial judges. But that's TV, not real life. In real life, doing so can easily come back to bite the lawyer right in the old *cojones*. This particular trial judge, who didn't sustain the objection, was John Crowley, a man with whom I had become very friendly dating back to when he was a misdemeanor court judge and I was assigned to his courtroom. Judge Crowley and his wife, Bette, had even been guests at my wedding the year before I was assigned to his felony trial courtroom at the Criminal Court Building.

Had I been prosecuting this case in front of a judge who, for any reason or no reason, didn't like and respect me, I could've easily gotten jammed by his sustaining the objection. This isn't to imply that trial attorneys need to kiss judges' asses, but neither should they antagonize them by, say, showing up in court wearing a garish maroon tuxedo with wide lapels, like Joe Pesci in *My Cousin Vinny*, or treating them as the enemy.

My Cousin Vinny, in its way, captures the often (dark) humorous spirit of the criminal justice system better than I've ever seen on the big screen, and it is my second favorite lawyer movie. My top pick is Otto Preminger's *Anatomy of a Murder*, in which James Stewart plays a criminal defense lawyer and George C. Scott plays a prosecutor. Written by a Michigan state trial judge, based on a true story, and filmed on location in the Upper Peninsula, *Anatomy* best captures the gravity of a big-time murder trial. Like *The Defenders*, in both films, the lawyers treat each other with respect. Neither the prosecution nor the defense is portrayed as the bad guy. Everyone is just doing their job to see that justice is done.

The summer between my second and third years of law school, I was a law clerk for the Cook County State's Attorney's Office, assigned to Judge Frank Machala's courtroom at the Criminal Court Building on the Southwest Side of Chicago. During my summer clerkship, I had the opportunity to conduct direct examination of prosecution witnesses, cross-examination of defense witnesses, and both opening and closing arguments.

In a letter he wrote on my behalf, Judge Machala wrote, "After his graduation he tells me that he intends to seek employment with the prosecutor's office, work he seems to enjoy, although I have a feeling that he would be just as effective as a defense counsel. … At this time, while he has one more year of law school still ahead of him, I'd rate him well above 65% of the attorneys in private practice after several years of such work. He seems to be very able to think on his feet and is a very fine attorney even now."

After being assigned by Bill Dwyer, the 1st chair ASA in Judge

Machala's courtroom, to work up a file in a case involving the shooting of a Chicago Police Department sergeant named Richard Scanlon, I discovered an inexplicable anomaly in the physical evidence: Scanlon had been shot in the stomach when trying to separate the defendant, James Dixon, from another man with whom Dixon was fighting.

After the shot rang out, Scanlon exclaimed, "Which one of you guys shot me?"

We knew from independent witnesses that two shots had been fired: one that led neighbors to call the police and the other that wounded Scanlon. But Dixon's .22 revolver, which was recovered across the street from the shooting, had only one expended shell casing, along with an empty chamber and three live rounds in the cylinder. I could not make sense of this, and neither could my dad, whom I consulted in the belief that if anyone could solve this mystery, it was he. What possible reason would Dixon have for breaking open the cylinder of his revolver after firing the first shot and removing the spent shell casing?

When I told Bill about the anomaly, he said, "Well, I'm not trying this piece of shit." He offered the defendant, who had spent nearly a year in jail awaiting trial, a sweetheart plea: time served in return for a plea of guilty to a misdemeanor of "unlawful use of weapons." Dixon's lawyer, Michael J. Green, was reluctant to plead his client, who he insisted was innocent. But he was ethically bound to convey the offer to his client, who accepted it.

Later, while Bill and I were alone in Judge Machala's courtroom, we received an anonymous phone call informing us that Scanlon had accidentally "shot himself" with the pen gun he carried in his shirt pocket. Apparently, it had gone off while Scanlon was trying to separate Dixon from the man he was fighting with. (In the '50s and '60s, so-called pen guns—small caliber, single-shot guns that looked like pens—were advertised in men's magazines as spy gadgets and emergency self-defense pieces.)

Not only had Scanlon failed to inform the grand jury of what happened (which he must have realized as he was being transported to the hospital or soon thereafter), but he had called the Chicago Police Department Crime Lab to cancel the examination of his shirt, which would have revealed gun powder residue *inside* his pocket. We told Mike Green what had happened and that we were going to dismiss the charges. But before we did that, we needed to get the shirt back from Scanlon to use as evidence against him.

The shirt had been held for the past year in evidence by the CPD, and, right after the plea, Scanlon had asked for its return. Bill Dwyer told me to call Scanlon to tell him that the defendant was withdrawing his plea, so we needed the shirt returned for evidence at trial. To our surprise, Scanlon did return the shirt—right after laundering it. Even so, the CPD Crime Lab was still able to detect the gunpowder inside the pocket. And, when you were really looking for it, you could see the broken threads at the bottom of the pocket where the bullet had exited before it penetrated the shirt and Scanlon's rotund abdomen.

To avoid prison, Scanlon pled guilty to perjury. That led to his firing from the department and denial of his pension. James Dixon received a $50,000 settlement of his wrongful conviction claim. The case, which made the front pages of all the Chicago newspapers, was quite a learning experience for a rising third-year law student.

My performance as a law clerk led Bill Dwyer and Terry Ekl to go to bat for me for a full-time position as an assistant state's attorney: "Randy has performed, in an exceptionally competent manner, <u>every</u> function normally performed by a trial assistant. Randy has participated in several felony trials, both bench and jury, including the preparation and examination of witnesses during trial, and the giving of opening and closing arguments. In our opinion, Randy has demonstrated, at this stage of his career, more ability as a trial lawyer than many of the 'experienced' attorneys with whom we come in daily contact. … We strongly feel … that he will be one of the most outstanding trial attorneys ever to prosecute for this office."

Without the enthusiastic recommendation of these senior trial lawyers, I doubt I would have gotten the job. I will forever be grateful for the opportunities they gave me that summer, and for their advocacy on my behalf.

In the fall, I returned to Harvard, where I was enrolled in its innovative nine-hour intensive course consisting of (a) a classroom professional responsibility component, (b) a trial-advocacy component modeled on the curriculum of the National Institute for Trial Advocacy (NITA), and (c) a clinical component in which a fellow student prosecutor and I prosecuted misdemeanor cases in Middlesex County, which included Cambridge, under the watchful eye of Nick Littlefield, a former assistant U.S. attorney. Above all, Nick stressed the importance of preparation and, to that end, demonstrated what true preparation entailed.

Then, having landed the job as an assistant state's attorney that would begin in the fall, in the summer after graduation, I returned to the State's Attorney's Office as a law clerk while I studied for the bar.

With all this experience and training under my belt (which I discuss in even greater detail in *A Life for Liberty*), I was far more prepared to be a criminal prosecutor than most of my peers, having internalized two critically important lessons. First, the value of preparation. Second, the need to behave ethically. Like Alice Richmond, I, too, had to look at myself every morning in the mirror … and respect the man I saw looking back.

"Henry Brisbon Is a *Bad* Man"

ON SEPTEMBER 1, 1977, having passed the bar, I achieved my boyhood dream by being sworn in as a criminal prosecutor. My first assignment was to the chief judge's courtroom at 26th and California—known as "26th and Cal"—the neoclassical-style Criminal Court Building built in the late 1920s on the Southwest Side, where all felony arraignments for the City of Chicago are handled. Next to it was a newly constructed office tower that opened after I was a law clerk and to which the State's Attorney's offices moved from the second floor of the Criminal Court Building. Behind it stands the Cook County Jail.

Figure 9. 26th and California in 1981

Normally, a new hire would have to pay his dues in either traffic court, juvenile court, or appeals. (These days, you're assigned to all three.) But due to my previous stints as a law clerk at 26th Street, the supervisors had come to know me and decided I could forgo those entry-level assignments in favor of the unique assignment to the chief judge's courtroom.

In the chief judge's courtroom, my boss was Sam Grossman, a diminutive, elderly, but very spry Jewish man with a full head of silver hair who'd been there seemingly forever. Sam was always dapperly dressed, complete with pocket square. Everyone knew and loved Sam.

Judge Richard Fitzgerald was chief judge of the Criminal Division. Before me, everyone assigned the job of organizing the arraignments and all attendant paperwork essentially had to learn it from Sam while doing the job. Being a fellow Jew, Sam took a special interest in me. He asked if I would write a manual for all those who came after me, so as to shorten their learning curve. Years later, former students told me they saw my memo, which was then still in use.

Most of the work during those three months in Judge Fitzgerald's courtroom was unchallenging drudgery. Arraignments were in the morning, and in the afternoon, I had to prepare the paperwork for the following morning's arraignments. But because I was working out of 26th and Cal, ground zero for all the biggest criminal cases in Cook County, the huge advantage of this assignment was that I had time to watch a lot of criminal trials.

In particular, I studied how prosecutors conducted their direct questioning, their cross-examinations, and their opening and closing arguments. Seeing what worked and what didn't, both style and substance, would be invaluable when I finally reached the felony trial courts. For example, in October, I got to watch Michael Ficaro give the closing argument in the trial of Henry Brisbon Jr., the so-called "I-57 murderer," who was charged with murdering a Chicago businessman and his fiancée in 1973. Ficaro was the chief of the Felony Trial Division of the State's Attorney's Office, and down the line, he would play an important role in my upward movement through the office.

Brisbon and his gang had a particular modus operandi. They would drive onto the interstate, get behind a car, and bump it, creating an accident that necessitated both cars exiting the interstate in the middle of nowhere under the pretext of exchanging information. In this case, they took the couple out of their car at gunpoint, led them to the middle of a cornfield, and laid them on their stomachs. The man and woman begged to be spared; they were going to be married in just six months. Hearing that, Brisbon told them, "Kiss your last kiss," and when they did, he fired a shotgun into their backs, murdering them.

Just an hour earlier, the gang had taken a woman from her car before making her strip naked and climb through a barbed wire fence at the side of the road. As she pleaded for her life, Brisbon put his shotgun up her vagina and pulled the trigger. Brisbon looked on as the woman suffered, then ended her life by shooting her in the neck. This was a guy for whom those with a moral conscience hope Hell exists—and if they believe it doesn't exist, they usually entertain fantasies of seeing done to him what he'd done to his victims.

Sentenced to death after his conviction, Brisbon declared as he left the courtroom, "You'll never get me. I'll kill again. Then you'll have another long trial. And then I'll do it again."

His plan was to keep killing so that the court would have to keep putting off his executions while he sat through new trials.

Good to his word, in the penitentiary at Stateville, he murdered an inmate named Richard Morgan. And as he predicted, Brisbon never was executed, becoming infamous in his own right among guards and inmates for his ferocity and taste for violence.

A few years after leaving the State's Attorney's Office to be a law professor, I was invited to be on a National Endowment for the Humanities program on criminal punishment, held at the Cook County Jail. The program consisted of a panel of professors discussing punishment theory. The audience was supposed to be comprised of one-third reporters, one-third community workers, and one-third inmates. But the first two groups didn't show up. So the whole audience was about 100 inmates in their tan jumpsuits sitting politely in rows of folding chairs.

To my astonishment, the other professors each read their scholarly papers as though presenting at the American Philosophical Association. When my turn came, I was introduced as a former Cook County State's Attorney. I thought it my duty to actually address the audience of inmates in the room. So I put aside my prepared remarks on the justice of restitution to victims of crime.

"Each of you are here because you did something bad," I said, and held out my two hands, palms down, even with each other. "Here is you, and here is your victim. You started out even." I lowered my left hand. "When you committed your crime, you lowered your victim. There are two ways to get justice for what you did. We can lower you down to the level of the victim. That is called 'punishment.'" I lowered my right hand until they were even again at a lower level in front of my chest, then raised my right hand again. "Or we can make you raise your victims up by making compensation to them." Now I raised my left hand until it was even with my right. "This is called 'restitution.'"

I sat down. When the presentations were done, it was time for questions from the audience. Some of the inmates formed a queue at the mic. Most of them complained about conditions at the jail. Then a much older African American inmate took the mic and said, "The state's attorney says we are here because we are bad. But there ain't no such thing as a bad man. We are only what society has made us."

The inmates may not have known what philosophy or a law professor was, but they sure knew what a state's attorney did. I thought, *How can I possibly have a productive debate with this guy?* And, more important, *How can I possibly win it?*

Now seated at a table on the dais, I leaned forward into the microphone in front of me: "What about Henry *Brisbane*?" I asked, knowing Brisbon's reputation among inmates as a stone-cold killer. (For whatever reason, I always heard prosecutors pronounce his name like the city in Australia.)

Figure 10. Henry Brisbon Jr. *(Courtesy of Illinois Department of Corrections)*

"Oh, you mean Henry *Brisbon*," the man corrected me, pronouncing it "Briz-bn." He then paused, thought for a moment, and replied: "Henry Brisbon … He's a *bad* man." And that ended our exchange.

My Friend Terry

AFTER THREE MONTHS in the chief judge's courtroom shuffling papers—but also learning by watching others try felony cases—I was transferred to the 1st Municipal Division of the Circuit Court of Cook County. The 1st Municipal handled all misdemeanors committed in the City of Chicago in branch courts located throughout the city—except for cases involving car thefts or drugs, which went to specialized courtrooms to which I was later assigned as well.

As I left Judge Fitzgerald and Sam Grossman, I was tasked with training my replacement, Terrence Hake. I did not socialize with many of my fellow prosecutors. The exception was Terry. He was a Loyola Law School graduate who was both modest and good-looking in a choir-boy sort of way.

Terry and I were sworn in as prosecutors on the same day in 1977, though we were not sworn in together. I took my oath with the other prosecutors who started on September 1, 1977, and was then assigned to the chief judge's court. Not Terry. He had clerked for the big boss, Mike Ficaro, who was working the I-57 murder heater case. In fact, Terry missed the mass ceremony and was sworn in by Ficaro while surveying the crime scene.

Ficaro wanted Terry to stick with him till Henry Brisbon's trial ended, which it did in mid-November. The Brisbon trial put Terry about two to three months behind me on the promotion scale. Whenever I advanced to the next level on my way to being a felony trial assistant, he would follow a couple months later, and I would give him the lay of the land. Because we were held in high regard by the bosses—me because of my successful clerkships at 26th Street, Terry because of his work with Mike Ficaro—he succeeded me in the chief judge's courtroom, where we first met. By bypassing traffic court, juvenile, and appeals, we were both on a privileged path to the felony trial courts.

As we rose up through the misdemeanor and preliminary hearing courtrooms together and then worked on Felony Review, Terry and I hung out often, enjoying drinks, dinners, lunches, and Northwestern basketball games (even though he was a Loyola grad). We once took a trip to Florida where we met up with another prosecutor, Bruce Paynter (whose father directed the Northwestern Wildcat Marching Band when I was an undergrad there). There we watched the Pittsburgh Pirates play a spring-training game. Terry and I also got horribly seasick on a fishing boat. Both of us ended up lying prone below deck, trying not to throw up into the buckets helpfully placed on the floor next to us by the crew.

Figures 11–14. Terry and me fishing and trying not to barf in Florida; spring training with ASA Bruce Paynter

Figure 15. Randy Barnett in Florida

Good times—we had lots of them. And in 1979, Terry would be a groomsman at my wedding to Beth.

With my transfer to the 1st Municipal Division, my career as a real prosecutor began.

"You Have the Mayor Call Me"

WHEN I MOVED from the felony arraignment court to the 1st Municipal Division, my first assignment was in Branch 43, located at Harrison and Kedzie on the West Side of Chicago.

Figure 16. Branch 43 at Harrison and Kedzie

The court was presided over by Judge John J. Crowley, an old, white-haired, cantankerous judge whom I've already mentioned and with whom I'd establish a close relationship during my time assigned to Branch 43.

Before becoming a judge, he'd been a civil trial lawyer for the City of Chicago in the Corporation Counsel's Office. So, unlike a lot of judges, he'd tried plenty of cases and understood the tactics and demands from both sides. Once upon a time, the clout from those connections had been enough to get him a decent assignment as a circuit court judge. Alas, whoever had been his clout died, and he was now perpetually stuck in the misdemeanor branch courts.

Figure 17. John Crowley *(center)* at boxing match

Crowley was known by prosecutors to be short-tempered. I was being sent into Branch 43 after he had kicked out another state's attorney for some unknown affront. I'd never been in a misdemeanor branch court before this assignment, had no idea what to expect, and was wholly unprepared for this experience out of Dante.

If you are old enough to remember the courtroom scenes in *Hill Street Blues*, you have an inkling of the kind of chaos that didn't at all resemble the solemnity of the criminal courts I'd experienced at 26th and California. Here, people were packed in elbow to elbow for the eighty cases a day—meaning eighty defendants, eighty groups of friends and family and lawyers, as well as eighty sets of victims, witnesses, and cops, all of them jostling and jockeying for air and space. All of them watching the "show" being performed by the judge and the attorneys appearing before him, wondering what would happen when their case was called.

The more senior prosecutor assigned to Branch 43 on that first day was Rebecca "Becky" Davidson, a former public defender who'd become a prosecutor. Somehow, I found her in the scrum. Becky could sense my bewilderment and said, "Don't worry. Just watch me and do what I do; follow my lead."

That lasted about twenty minutes, if that long.

Becky then handed me a bunch of files—a "file" being the one-page form complaint the arresting officer fills out, along with a two- or three-page arrest report.

"Do these," she said.

Do what to them?

I was supposed to evaluate the cases, decide how to proceed in front of the judge, and, since these were misdemeanors, negotiate with the defense attorneys about a plea bargain in order to get them off the docket. The problem was that penalties on misdemeanors ranged from supervision (which could be expunged) to probation (which is a conviction that couldn't be) to a full year in county jail. And in some of these files, I could hardly tell what the crime was by reading the sketchily described facts of the case. I certainly had no sense whatsoever of what penalty these crimes deserved or ordinarily received. Nor did I appreciate the fact that, mixed in with these garden-variety misdemeanors, there were some more serious-sounding complaints that Felony Review had rejected.

In the misdemeanor cases I'd helped try back in Cambridge, my supervisor Nick Littlefield had stressed the importance of preparation:

"Start with the elements and the proof of each element, anticipate the legal and factual problems and defenses, and structure the presentation of the case to cut off the defense." Then investigation: "Track down the answer to each factual problem, find every piece of evidence and every witness, do it yourself ('like a whirlwind')." Finally, organization: Organize your case "around a written trial brief."

And he had warned me about the demands placed on line prosecutors: "I hope in Chicago that the lesson I thought you learned about preparation over the semester will not be forgotten in the pressure of a heavy case load and the accepted practice among overloaded city prosecutors of trying cases cold from the files."

All that excellent advice? It had now been rendered moot on day one. Which is not to say it disappeared from my conscience. Whenever I acted contrary to his advice, I could hear Nick's voice whispering in my ear and felt guilty. And when the time came to try felony cases, I tried as best I could to hew to his wisdom, however imperfectly.

But now, here I was in front of Judge Crowley and beside the defense attorney, presumably a public defender, representing the people of Cook County on a case of small import. But for me at that moment, it might as well have been O. J.'s trial.

All of my years performing on stages as a young musician or a debater hadn't quite prepared me for this moment. Neither had my training at Harvard Law School. *What do I do when I can't do what I know I am supposed to do?*

Most of that day and the days that followed are a blur. But I remember one case in particular. I was standing in front of the bench with my back to the audience in the packed courtroom. After looking over his copy of "the file," Crowley threw the sheets in my direction, where they scattered on his bench. (Crowley was said to throw case files at the prosecutor, and I now knew those tales were sort of true.)

"Mr. State's Attorney," he barked, then paused before demanding, "what're you going to do about this?"

Do about what? What was the issue? Did the complaint misstate the law? Had the cops tried to pull a fast one? I had absolutely no idea what he could've been referring to.

The judge, who after decades in the belly of the beast could spot bullshit at the speed of light, had determined something that I couldn't see.

In the millisecond that followed, I conducted an internal cost-benefit analysis and made a fateful and potentially disastrous decision. I decided to follow the judge's lead. I would do what he wanted me to do. This was a complete abdication of my responsibility as a prosecutor. And, given the level of corruption in the Circuit Court of Cook County, it was also extraordinarily risky. But Crowley was not known to be corrupt. And he seemed to be the only one in the place who knew what was going on. So I went with my gut and also my judgment of character.

Instinct and luck turned out to be on my side.

I said, "Motion state S.O.L."—which stands for Stricken Off with Leave to Reinstate. This meant I was moving to dismiss the case but asking to reserve the right to reinstate the charge within the statute of limitations (which virtually never happened). I then held my breath for what might be coming.

If I'd mis-inferred the meaning of "What're you going to do about this?," I'd know right away. But the look on his face and his body language said I'd done what he had wanted me to do.

"What are you going to do about this?" was his coded signal that something was wrong with the charge or the evidence supporting it. Or, as he often put it when away from the bench, "It was bullshit." In court, he'd rarely get to the specifics of what that something was, just as law school professors using the Socratic method did not come out and tell you the answer; you had to guess their thought processes. Eventually, thanks to Judge Crowley, I came to understand exactly what was wrong with a case and could spot it myself before appearing before him.

During the three months I was assigned to the chief judge's courtroom doing felony arraignments, I held the title of assistant state's attorney. But it was under the tutelage of John Crowley on the West Side of Chicago that I began the process of becoming a *real* prosecutor.

Many times, I would sit with Crowley in his spartan chambers during recesses or after the court day was completed for explanations and tutoring. He knew the law. He kept up with the case law. Most important, he understood the structure of the law and the proper role of a judge in administering justice, which was, after all, what the prosecutor was supposed to be doing, too. In the weeks that followed, I never knowingly brought a case to the bench that couldn't pass muster with him.

Judge Crowley's most peculiar idiosyncrasy was that he didn't like to drive himself to work. He was known to have court personnel pick him up from his condo on Lake Shore Drive overlooking Lake Michigan. Can't say that I blamed him. It was a long schlep from the lake to the branch court at Harrison and Kedzie on the West Side. As it happened, I lived just a few blocks north of him in a 3rd-floor walk-up on Bittersweet Place in the Uptown neighborhood, just off Lake Shore Drive and one block north of Irving Park Road. (In Latin Eagles territory, as I noted earlier.) Crowley not so subtly suggested that maybe I should drive him to work. Which I was delighted to do in my Dodge Diplomat, and I often picked him up, giving us lots of time to talk.

People sometimes tell you things in the car on long drives, possibly because of the proximity, that they'd normally not say in ordinary conversation. For instance, he'd met his wife, Bette, he said, when he was a trial lawyer in the Corporation Counsel's Office, which represented the City of Chicago in its civil litigation. Bette was one of the prospective jurors in a case he was trying. Crowley leaned over to his partner and told him, "Look at the boobs on that one. Let's keep her on the jury."

Now I realize that the prosecutor driving the judge to and from work every day sounds fishy. But that's the thing about an honest judge. It had no effect on how he did his job. He was always prepared to ream me out publicly if he thought I was screwing up. And it certainly did not affect the disposition of any case. That would also be true of the first judge to whom I was assigned as a felony assistant at 26th and Cal. (More on that judge later.)

In all my years as an assistant state's attorney, my four months in Branch 43 in John Crowley's courtroom might well have been the most valuable of my legal career. It was there that I learned how to spot the bullshit, and to stand my ground against the pressures of the cops, lawyers, and witnesses, and to stand up even to him. And it was important that I see just how an honest judge could operate in a corrupt system.

"You know, Randy," he told me one day in his chambers. "I get phone calls all the time about the cases on my call. They say, 'Judge, the mayor is interested in this case.' And I always tell them, 'Fine, you have the mayor call me.' You know, in all the time I've been on this bench, the mayor has never called me."

Judge Thomas J. Maloney

JUDGES SOMETIMES TAKE vacations, and Judge Crowley enjoyed his. During one such vacation, he was temporarily replaced by Circuit Judge Thomas J. Maloney. As a young man, Maloney had been a boxer, and he looked like an Irish pugilist. He'd begun the practice of law the year I was born, 1952. When I appeared before him in Branch 43, he'd only recently been appointed a circuit court judge by the Illinois Supreme Court.

Unlike some other criminal court judges, Maloney had been a skilled criminal defense lawyer who knew how to try cases. He ran an efficient trial and was clearly in command of the room. Some judges have that demeanor of authority. But Maloney was imbued with it.

By the time he arrived, I was on top of the job as a misdemeanor branch court prosecutor. The funny thing about rising up through the ranks is that you start an assignment completely lost, eventually catch on to become the master of that particular domain, and then get promoted to another assignment in which you are lost all over again. It is like going from a know-it-all senior in high school to a clueless freshman in college, and then from a confident senior in college to an insecure first-year law student.

One case in front of Maloney stands out in memory. It involved a young woman who had been assaulted by her ex-boyfriend. When the case was called, the complainant was not in the courtroom. The defendant was on bond and stood next to his public defender in front of the bench. The judge asked if I was ready for trial, but I obviously wasn't. So the public defender asked that the complaint be dismissed. In a high-volume misdemeanor courtroom, this would not have been unusual. But given the seriousness of the charges, I thought that was premature. I asked Judge Maloney for time to try to contact the complainant. He agreed.

During a break in the action, I went back to the judge's chamber and used his phone to call the complainant's number listed on the police report. She answered. I identified myself and asked why she had not shown up in court. She said that the defendant had come to her apartment and attempted to force his way in by removing a window screen, then threatened to beat her if she testified against him. I gave her the number of the courtroom in case she needed to reach me.

I returned to the courtroom and had the case recalled. With the defendant and his lawyer standing before the court, I informed the judge of what the complainant told me and asked that the defendant's bond be revoked and he be taken into custody, to which the public defender objected. Much to my surprise, Judge Maloney did not hesitate (unlike many misdemeanor court judges). He ordered the bailiff to take the defendant into custody, and a trial date was set. The defendant was led away to the lockup.

Not long after, one of the courtroom personnel told me there was a phone call for me. It was the complainant who was now crying and yelling at me. "I did not know you were going to take him into custody. I did not want that. I love him." What? How could she possibly know what had just happened?

She knew because the defendant was given a phone call on his way to the detention cell, and he'd called her. She then called me at the number I'd given her. I told her I was going to come see her after the court adjourned. When court ended, I drove to her apartment. We talked. Her mother was also present. What she said satisfied me that her current attitude hadn't been coerced, and I told her I would see that the charges were dropped. But I explained to her in plain language the consequences of using the criminal justice system to punish her boyfriend, then changing her mind later.

I was pissed at being put in the position of making a representation to a judge I had just met, only to find out that my representation was likely false. How would that judge trust me in the future? This was my fault. What I had overlooked on the misdemeanor complaint was that felony charges had been rejected by our Felony Review Unit. Having not yet experienced Felony Review, I didn't understand what a rejection indicated about the case, which was usually that it was, as John Crowley would say, "bullshit."

The next day, upon arriving at Harrison and Kedzie, I went to speak to Judge Maloney in his chambers. I recounted my visit to the complainant's home and told him I intended to writ the defendant to the courtroom from the Cook County Jail to appear the next day, intending to drop all charges. I apologized for misleading the court.

He told me I had done no such thing. In fact, he said, I had done the right thing both in reaching out to the victim before dropping the charges and in seeking to have the defendant's bond revoked. What most impressed him was my visiting the complainant in person—something that was not really done in misdemeanor cases—and then promptly informing him of the situation and of my intent to drop charges against the defendant.

What impressed me was Tom Maloney. He was, I thought, a stand-up judge. I would later try two felony jury trials before him after he'd been assigned to 26th and Cal.

But as I learned much later, he was not the judge I thought he was.

"Any Day Now I Expect the Feds to Be Crashing Down the Door"

FROM BRANCH 43, I moved to Branch 46, home to the two courtrooms where all the misdemeanor jury trials in Chicago were held. It was thanks to Branch 46 that corrupt lawyers were able to get around honest misdemeanor branch court judges like John Crowley. If they had a case in front of an honest judge that they wanted to fix, they would demand a jury, and their case would automatically be transferred to Branch 46. Fittingly, these courtrooms were located in the traffic court building right on the Chicago River at LaSalle Street. I say fittingly because traffic court was notoriously corrupt, and Branch 46 was, too.

Everyone in the legal system knew that you could probably get your case fixed in traffic court. Here's what I knew: My dad told my mom (and later me) that, if she ever was stopped by a Chicago police officer for a traffic violation, she should ask the officer if he knew Bob Sinnocrak. Sinnocrak was a Chicago police sergeant assigned to the Traffic Division whose beat included my dad's laundry on the South Side.

Sinnocrak typically rode a three-wheel motorcycle as he handed out parking tickets. He was also quite a character and a bit of a hard-ass. When he was upbraided for writing a parking ticket to a car parked near some politically connected location, he responded by ticketing all the illegally parked cars outside the police district station. Or something like that. The details are a little fuzzy, but the gist of that story made quite an impression on my dad and on me.

One time, my mom was stopped for speeding. But she could not remember Bob Sinnocrak's name, which was understandable. So when she came home with a speeding ticket, my dad got upset: "Why didn't you mention Bob Sinnocrak?"

Dad accompanied Mom to traffic court and told the arresting officer that he knew Bob Sinnocrak. The officer then instructed my mom that her case would be held to the end of the court call and that, when it was called, she should tell the judge that she was "just keeping up with traffic." After most everyone else had left the courtroom, Mom's case was called, and she stood before the judge on the bench. The officer testified about her speeding, and then the judge asked my mom for her side of the story. She told him that she was just keeping up with traffic. That must have been the code word for the day, since the judge then immediately dismissed the violation.

Stories like that from my dad are how I learned about traffic court and how things worked in Chicago. Those stories are also why I was pleasantly surprised by the absence of even a hint of corruption in the Cook County State's Attorney's Office.

Two judges presided over the two jury trial courtrooms in Branch 46: John "Gentleman Jack" Reynolds and John J. ("JJ") McDonnell. After one or the other judge had been bribed, the lawyers would then waive their client's right to a jury, whereby the client would either be acquitted at a fixed bench trial or, more often, receive a sweetheart sentence like supervision after pleading guilty.

The two judges were said to dislike each other because they competed for bribes. I remember sitting with JJ in his dimly lit chambers as he held a stogie and said, "You know that Jack Reynolds is such a kink. Any day now I expect the feds to be crashing down the door." JJ must've figured that, by talking to me like that, I wouldn't think *he* was just as corrupt as Reynolds.

JJ loved telling stories. One day after the court call, he regaled me with one about how he had gotten a flat tire in a sketchy neighborhood on the West Side. While he waited for the auto club to deal with it, tactical police officers in an unmarked car pulled over and stopped a car of young Hispanic men. All occupants were ordered out of their car and made to sit down on the side of the road while the officers ransacked the car looking for contraband—whether drugs or guns or both. While this was happening, he slunk down in the driver's seat so no one would see him there. Finding nothing criminal, the cops got back into their cruiser and left the scene.

This story stuck with me. In our criminal justice system, the only practical remedy for police misconduct is the exclusionary rule. Under that rule, evidence of criminality is "suppressed" or excluded from a trial if it is the product of an illegal search. The exclusionary rule only kicks in when there is evidence of guilt that a prosecutor later seeks to use against the accused. So this remedy can generally be asserted only by those who are guilty of wrongdoing.

In J J's story, the cops found no evidence of criminal conduct that might later be suppressed. So those Hispanic youths were both innocent of any wrongdoing and without any practical legal remedy for the illegal search. And yet they were subjected to the indignity of what was likely a search for which "probable cause" would be contrived after contraband was found (for example, a taillight broken by the cops themselves).

This insight contributed to my first law review article as a law professor: "Resolving the Dilemma of the Exclusionary Rule: An Application of Restitutive Principles of Justice," published in the *Emory Law Journal.* In that 1983 article, I advocated replacing the exclusionary rule with a system of restitution for police misconduct in which any citizen—guilty or innocent—can seek monetary damages from the police department. I explain the many reasons why the systematic availability of a restitution remedy is likely to deter police misconduct better than excluding evidence of guilt.

While the article was widely neglected, in part because I became a contracts and not a criminal law professor, I still believe its reasoning is sound. Some years later, Yale law professor Akhil Reed Amar got considerable attention for making the same proposal in his book *The Constitution and Criminal Procedure: First Principles* (1997).

In addition to Branch 46 being where I appeared before my first corrupt judges, it was also where I tried the only jury trial I ever lost—marring my otherwise perfect record—one of the two I tried there with fellow prosecutor Mark Rakoczy. (Later on, I also had one hung jury as a felony trial assistant, but that was not an *L.*) Mark and I would soon partner again.

The Judge May Be Coming Back Early from Vacation

MY NEXT STOP after Branch 46 was Branch 64, auto theft court, which was located in the Chicago Police Department's thirteen-story headquarters building at 11th and State—eleven blocks south of the center of downtown Chicago. Built in 1928, the building housed the pioneering Chicago Police Department Crime Lab.

It was also where, in the 1960s, John E. Reid developed polygraph techniques for the Chicago Police Department. Reid's approach focused on combining the use of a polygraph with interrogation methods that supposedly revealed deception. His approach became widely used in law enforcement across the United States, though critics came to believe that the results of his examinations were more influenced by his dubious questioning method than the results of "the box." By the time I was an ASA, Reid had his own well-known private polygraph firm.

During its last years of operation, the office of the Film Review Board, founded in 1907 as the Police Censor Board, was located on the 8th floor. A 2024 article in the *Saturday Evening Post* credits Chicago as "the first city to take action against the film industry" when "the city enacted a local government code requiring film distributors to submit their movies to a board for review." The Police Censor Board "was one of the most notorious of the movie monitors. Throughout its tenure in the film oversight business ... the board made many strange and arbitrary choices and let itself be corrupted at almost every turn. And yet it laid the groundwork for the movie ratings we know today."

In 2014, the *Chicago Tribune* reported that, at 11th and State, "the movies were kept in a vault before being screened in a projection room with thick walls. That was necessary, as Cmdr. John Kennedy told the Tribune many years later, 'so no one could hear the huffing and puffing from the dirty movies.'" However, the board did not limit itself to censoring the sounds of pornography. For example, a 1931 travelogue starring Douglas Fairbanks entitled "Around the World in 80 Minutes" was censored for an aerial view of Chicago. "I wonder what city this is," says a voice, followed by "the sound of gunshots" and a different voice saying, "Oh, yes. This is Chicago."

Sounds like parts of Chicago today.

The Branch 64 courtroom was located on the 10th floor. The presiding judge was John Devine, who'd previously been a traffic court judge. This court handled all trials for misdemeanors involving cars, like criminal trespass to vehicles. Those were trials ending in conviction or acquittal, just like in Branch 43. Unlike Branch 43, however, Branch 64 also held preliminary hearings for all felony charges involving auto crime, such as auto theft.

Figure 18. Chicago Police Department Headquarters at 11th and State

This was my first opportunity to handle felony cases.

In Illinois, there were two ways to bring felony charges: by indictment or by information. An indictment was issued by the grand jury located at 26th and California upon a finding of probable cause reached after a confidential hearing. When I was a felony trial assistant, I presented several cases of my own to the grand jury for an indictment. Most felony charges, however, are brought by information rather than by indictment, after finding of probable cause by a judge at a public preliminary hearing. Once an "information" is issued by the judge, the case is then referred to a felony trial court.

The bulk of the cases in Branch 64 were low level misdemeanors involving joyriding in or damage to cars. But on occasion we would hold a preliminary hearing for a felony, such as what is now widely known as "grand theft auto" due to the video game of the same name. Our biggest cases involved so-called "chop shops." In the hierarchy of auto theft cases, it didn't get any higher than a chop shop—the colloquial term for the garages where stolen cars were taken to be chopped into parts, from mufflers to headlights to transmissions, and so forth, for resale in used-car wrecking yards and elsewhere. I vividly recall going with my dad to a wrecking yard in Hammond, Indiana, to get used parts to fix our cars.

Selling stolen cars whole (unchopped) was risky because every car since the 1960s has had its own vehicle identification number, or "VIN."

By and large, unless you send them intact to third-world countries, stolen cars are mostly worthless because of the vehicle ID numbers located in a few places on the car, from the engine block to the chassis. But the individual parts of a car do not have numbers. Once a car is disassembled into its parts, these parts can then be sold by auto parts yards at a considerable profit. And auto parts yards in Chicago were controlled by organized crime, as were the chop shops that fed them illicit parts. Whenever a chop shop was busted by auto theft detectives, the cases would end up in this court. In Branch 64, a chop shop case was the equivalent of a murder-one case.

My first partner in Branch 64 was Mark Rakoczy, with whom I had tried misdemeanor jury trials in Branch 46 in front of the corrupt Judges Jack Reynolds and JJ McDonnell. Now he and I were making the state's case at a preliminary hearing about whether the owners of a chop shop who'd been arrested by the Chicago PD's specialized Auto Theft Unit would face trial.

To appreciate what happened during this particular chop shop preliminary hearing, it is important to know that Judge Devine's normal policy was not to allow any motions to suppress for illegal searches and seizures. If a defense attorney moved to suppress a piece of evidence, Judge Devine rejected the motion, informing the attorney that such a motion was premature during the probable-cause hearing. Instead, he said, the motion should be filed in whatever trial court the case was assigned after probable cause was found.

"Objection. Beyond the scope of preliminary hearing," we'd say.

"Sustained," Judge Devine would invariably respond.

In one particular case, Mark was the lead prosecutor. I stood beside him in front of the judge's bench as he put on the direct testimony of a Chicago police officer from the CPD Auto Theft Unit that had organized the chop shop raid. It was all relatively informal. The cop stood before the bench, rather than in a witness box, while Mark questioned him.

The defense lawyer for the chop shop guys was "Eddie" Genson, a well-known Chicago defense attorney. Edward Marvin Genson would later represent musician R. Kelly and newspaper owner Conrad Black. A graduate of Northwestern Law School, he became an adjunct professor at the Chicago-Kent College of Law when I was on the faculty there.

In 2007, *Chicago Magazine* featured him in a flattering profile complete with a striking photograph of him at his desk. In 2008, some thirty years after I faced him in Branch 64, I was surprised to see him on television accompanying his client, Illinois Governor Rod "Blago" Blagojevich, whom the federal government was prosecuting for corruption. Despite Eddie's representation, Blago was convicted, and his sentence was commuted years later by President Trump.

On this day in 1978, Eddie Genson was fixing a case in Branch 64.

The defendant, James Beil, was arrested at a two-car brick garage located at 4821 South Keeler. Genson filed a motion to suppress, alleging various false allegations in the police report and that the complaint for the search warrant did "not set forth sufficient facts to justify a finding of probable cause for the issuance of the search warrant in this cause." We were not concerned about the motion, as that would be considered later by the trial judge after a finding of probable cause by Judge Devine.

Figure 19. Eddie Genson
(courtesy of Tom Maday)

During direct examination, the arresting officer explained the circumstances of the raid and what was found. It all sounded like standard operating procedure. Then it was Genson's turn to cross-examine. He started to ask the cop questions about the circumstances surrounding the legal basis of the search that led to the arrest, which my partner and I knew Judge Devine didn't allow.

"Objection, Judge," Mark said. "Beyond the scope of preliminary hearing."

"Overruled."

Overruled? Well, that had never happened before.

Okay, so now the cop began describing circumstances that sounded like he and his team hadn't had probable cause for the search, giving far more details without being prompted than he would have if he were trying to elide the truth. If police officers ever lie about searches and arrests, it is to make them seem *legal*; they don't freely volunteer evidence of illegality. Why would he do that?

The only reasonable inference there was—well, you know. In the State's Attorney's Office, we'd been instructed to look for cases like this, with police reports that describe the circumstances of the search in vague terms. Such reports created an opening for a defendant to make a motion to suppress and walk free thanks to a paid-off cop testifying to or admitting to unconstitutional searches: ergo, case dismissed. It was an ingenious way of fixing cases before they ever got to trial.

So we immediately knew we had a dirty cop. But we also knew one more thing: We had a dirty judge. Why else would he have changed his normal procedures to allow this line of questioning? Devine was obviously in on the whole charade. Only later did we learn that John Devine's nickname as a traffic court judge was "Dollars" Devine. That would have been handy to know.

This situation also illustrates one of the benefits of the "rule of law," which requires that "like cases be treated alike." Any deviation from that norm is a potential signal of something improper. It did not matter what policy Judge Devine had adopted for taking evidence on the illegality of a search or arrests. He could have had a policy of hearing such motions or not. What tipped us off was that he uncharacteristically *deviated* from the policy he had established.

At the end of Genson's cross-examination of the cop, Judge Devine declared, "Finding of no probable cause." Meaning no trial. End of case.

My partner, Mark, stormed off into the State's Attorney's office, located to the left of and behind the bench. Mark slammed the heavy, old wooden door to our office so hard that everyone in the courtroom could hear it. As I stood in front of the bench, I looked up at Judge Devine, who had a grin on his face as he uttered words I'll never forget:

"I think," he said, "my buddy is mad at me."

Mark wasn't the only one who was irate. Even in Branch 46 misdemeanor jury court, I had never had a case fixed out from under me like this. In Branch 46, a defendant in a fixed case would typically plead guilty and get supervision and eventual expungement of the conviction. I had never tried a fixed bench trial there. I was pissed.

More than pissed. I was uncontrollably angry.

At the end of that morning court session, when I could not get myself to calm down, I went into the office of my supervisor, Dennis Cooley, and told him what had happened. Dennis had been a Chicago police officer who'd gone to law school at night. In terms of demeanor, he was still much more street cop than lawyer. If you'd never seen him try a case as a felony trial assistant—I had when I was assigned to the chief judge's court at 26th Street—you'd wonder whether he actually knew what he was doing. He did. His brusque, down-to-earth manner appealed to jurors.

I told Dennis that I was as furious as I'd ever been and needed some advice on how to get my equilibrium back.

"If you give me a reason to calm down," I said, "I think I can."

"Okay," he said. "Here's a good reason. If Eddie Genson ever gets the idea that you have it in for him like this, he'll use it against you. Someday down the road, you'll go to trial again against him, and if you take a particular position in court that he knows is going to hurt him, he'll tell the judge, 'The state's attorney is doing this not because he thinks it's right, but because he has a thing against me, and everybody knows it.' That might be enough for the judge to rule against you."

"Thanks, Dennis," I said, "that's all I needed to hear." And I calmed down, remembering the adage, "Don't get mad, get even."

But when would I ever have that opportunity?

That was answered by another adage: "What goes around comes around." In other jurisdictions, the expression is "the wheel turns." Sure enough, about six weeks later, the wheel turned.

Chop shops were big stories in the local media. One evening, I saw on the news that another chop shop had been busted. So I knew the case would be coming to me eventually. In court the next day, after the morning call, I went into my office to eat my lunch. The phone rang. It was Eddie Genson.

"Are you the assistant that's going to be handling the chop shop case tomorrow?"

"Yeah."

"Well, that's my case. I'm just calling to see if you will be ready for hearing tomorrow."

There was a sensible reason why a lawyer might ask that when working on cases like this. Prosecuting a chop shop case required tedious paperwork involving tedious details like matching vehicle identification numbers. The state's attorneys usually took one continuance for a couple of weeks to ensure that all the charging documents were in order. Genson knew this was standard practice.

But now I knew Eddie Genson, whom I hadn't seen since the day he fixed the last big chop shop case, was going to be the lawyer. I also knew that Judge Devine happened to be on vacation that week, with a replacement judge on the bench. I'd seen the replacement judge that morning at the call. I knew nothing about him, but I decided I would rather take a chance on a judge I didn't know than one I knew to be dirty.

"Yes, Eddie," I said, "we'll be ready for the hearing tomorrow."

"Really?" he said. "I have all these witnesses I'm going to have to bring in, and I don't want to have to get everyone all worked up, only to have you ask for a continuance at the last second."

"Don't worry about that," I said. "Just be ready."

And now here it came.

"Look," he said, "I understand why you might not want to have this heard in front of Judge Devine." I had to stop myself from either laughing or gasping at the tacit admission. "But Judge Devine is on vacation now, right?"

"That's right."

"How long is he supposed to be on vacation?"

"Two weeks. This is his first week."

"Well, since he's going to be on vacation for two weeks, I won't object if you just want to get a one-week continuance, and then it'll be continued to next week, when he'll still be on vacation. I'll have time to prepare it, you'll have time to prepare, and everybody's happy. Okay?"

I listened to him and found myself tempted to say yes, agreeing that we'd still have a week with the replacement judge, but ixnay on that. If that's what Eddie wanted, there must be a reason.

"No, you be ready tomorrow," I said. "I'll call you if I change my mind."

"Really?" he pressed.

"Really," I said.

I hung up the phone, finished my lunch, and went back to the courtroom for the afternoon call. The court clerk, Chester—an older man, round-faced, weary, near retirement—was standing up behind his desk right next to the judge's bench, elevated, though not as high. To no one in particular, he said, "I was just talking to the judge on the phone, and he said he may be cutting his vacation short."

Yep, my instincts had been right.

The next day, Genson showed up to represent his client with not a single witness in tow and all but waived the preliminary hearing. Obviously, there was no reason to contest a preliminary hearing in front of an honest judge. Genson asked no questions of any witnesses, and that was that. The replacement judge made a finding of probable cause. What went around had come around. Sorry, Eddie.

"There's a Lot of Money to Be Made Out There, and I'm Ready to Make It"

AFTER THAT FIX, Mark and I started sending our chop shop cases directly to the grand jury to avoid any probable cause preliminary hearings in front of Devine. But chop shop cases were few and far between. "Dollars" Devine was engaged in corruption on a day-to-day basis.

The real money was not in big cases that might attract attention, but in small misdemeanor cases with defendants who were out on bond. Elsewhere in the United States, bonds are still issued by private bondsmen who vouch for the appearance of a defendant. In those places, you often see illuminated signs for "Bail Bonds" near downtown courthouses. If a defendant skips, the bondsman might find and haul him to court rather than forfeit the bond.

It can be an unsavory business. In Chicago, the county had taken over the bail bond system as a reform measure. To get released on, say, a $10,000 bond, a defendant needed to post 10 percent in cash, or $1,000. They would then receive a receipt for their payment, called a "bond slip." Should they appear in court as promised, the $1,000 deposit would be refunded to them at the end of their legal proceeding, win or lose. Or they could assign the bond to a family member.

Or to a lawyer.

In the hallways outside misdemeanor courts, lawyers would fish for clients who were out on bond. They would offer to represent them for "free" in return for the defendant signing over their bond slip. Most were much less than $1,000. Some were as low as $100, so the real money was made on volume. In front of a corrupt judge, a corrupt lawyer could also promise supervision or even possibly an acquittal if the complaining witness was not present. How could the lawyer know how the case would be disposed? Because he would split the bond with the judge.

I first came across this system in Branch 64. After Judge Devine issued a bond for a newly arrested defendant, he would tell the defendant to "see the bar lawyer." In Chicago, private lawyers would volunteer to represent clients pro bono under a program administered by the Chicago Bar Association. But when Judge Devine said "bar lawyer," he meant one of the kinky lawyers with whom he was splitting bonds. A "kink" was not a sexual term; it was how we referred to a crooked lawyer or judge. In other locales, they say "bent."

On the days when there was a real CBA bar lawyer in court, the judge would refer a case to that lawyer. Then, when the bar lawyer left the room with that client, Devine would set bond on a bunch of cases and quickly shuttle them to his favorite kink lawyer—a ruddy-faced, middle-aged man with jet black hair named Edward Kaplan. Whenever a bar lawyer showed up, I took it upon myself to explain to him this system and urged him to remain in the courtroom as much as possible.

After about three months in Branch 64, I was joined by my friend Terry Hake. The day Terry arrived—doing as I would have with anyone, not just a friend—I warned him about how crooked Judge Devine was and described how we bypassed him on big cases by taking them to the grand jury. So, unlike me, Terry was on notice from the get-go that Judge Devine was bent.

I trained another new prosecutor at Branch 64, an ASA I will call Matt. Matt was a good-looking, genial young man who always dressed well (not all ASAs or attorneys did). Unbeknownst to me at the time, Matt had become, or would become, even closer to Terry than I was. Indeed, they and their girlfriends would double-date.

At some point, Matt told me that he was leaving the State's Attorney's Office. I was surprised and asked him why. We hadn't even gotten to the felony trial courts yet. There was a lot more to learn on the job.

"Randy," he said, "there's a lot of money to be made out there, and I'm ready to make it."

Also unknown to me, Matt had become close to Judge Jack Reynolds, one of the two corrupt judges from Branch 46 misdemeanor jury court. Reynolds had been transferred to Branch 42, the felony preliminary hearing court located at Belmont and Western, to which I was later assigned after Felony Review. Sometime after he left the office, Matt joined up with the good-looking, sharp-dressing Tommy Del Beccaro, whom I knew when he was a public defender and who'd become a hallway bond-slip lawyer in Branch 42. Rumor had it that Tommy was even dating Jack Reynolds's daughter.

By this time, I was aware that a good portion of the crooked lawyers prowling the criminal courts were former assistant state's attorneys from the bad old days when the office was as political as everything else about Cook County. That led me to wonder who among my 550 fellow ASAs would end up being corrupt defense attorneys down the road. I had not expected clean-cut Matt to be one of them.

But I was soon to be presented with an even bigger and more demoralizing surprise.

* * *

One of the more bizarre occurrences I experienced as a prosecutor happened in Branch 64. After I arrived in the courtroom for the morning call, a huge African American jail guard in a neatly pressed blue uniform came into the State's Attorney's one-room office behind the bench to ask for my assistance. Also located on the 10th floor, adjacent to the courtroom, was an elevator transfer point for prisoners being shuttled between the lockup on the higher floors and the various branch courts on other floors of the building.

Sometime during the movement of prisoners, one of the prisoners was set upon by the others. This guard had segregated the suspects from the victim, putting them in a holding cell, and wanted me to get the suspects to admit what they had done. Here I was at five feet eleven, 160 pounds (as memorialized on my state's attorney's ID), with an NFL lineman of a guard standing behind me. I could not for the life of me imagine what I could say that would get them to talk. (I had yet to experience the interrogation of suspects in Felony Review, though in hindsight I don't think even that would have helped.) But I felt I owed it to the guard, who seemed to have faith that an authority figure in a suit and tie might command the respect of these arrestees. I didn't want to let him down.

Whatever it was I said, which I don't remember, wasn't working. And now, more and more prisoners were exiting the elevators. Before long, they began jamming the narrow corridor and squeezing the suspects the guards wanted kept separate. At last, I told the guard I didn't know what else to do. He shrugged his shoulders and thanked me for trying. And what struck me was how decent this man was for wanting to do something, anything, to rectify an injustice. No doubt he had worked in this capacity for years in Cook County, where doing nothing was standard operating procedure. And yet he'd wanted to try.

After several months in Branch 64, my next stop was Felony Review.

PART II: FELONY REVIEW

The Booking Reviewers

WHEN I WAS a junior at Northwestern, I became the advertising director of the *Chicago Reader*, a hip "free weekly" modeled after the *Boston Phoenix*. It was a great gig that ended up funding my Harvard Law education.

Six years later, in June 1979, the *Reader* assigned one of its top writers, Robert McClory, to do a profile of a unit in the State's Attorney's Office that I happened to be assigned to at the time. I'll let the headline—"The Booking Reviewers"—and subhead describe it: "In most American cities, decisions about whether or not to book felony charges are made by police. In Chicago, they are made by the State's Attorney's Felony Review team—a group of lawyers who are mostly young, often bright, and almost always on the firing line."

My favorite part of that description is "often bright."

It was a cover story and quite long, including on its front page a photo of me, in a suit, standing in front of an old, decommissioned police station with an ornate facade. Kathy Richland, the *Reader*'s well-known feature photographer, had taken me there to shoot my portrait. But my pose was not macho enough to fit the story. So Kathy instructed me exactly how to stand with my feet spread wide and pelvis thrust forward.

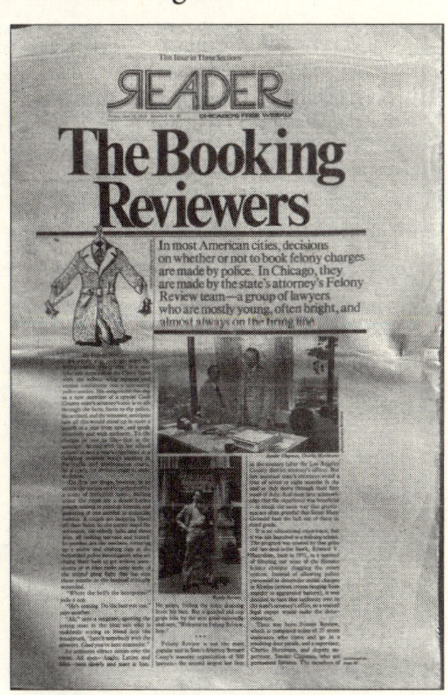

READER

The Booking Reviewers

In most American cities, decisions on whether or not to book felony charges are made by police. In Chicago, they are made by the state's attorney's Felony Review team—a group of lawyers who are mostly young, often bright, and almost always on the firing line.

Figure 20. Feature article about Felony Review *(courtesy of Chicago Reader)*

That I was working in Felony Review when this story appeared was no coincidence. After I joined the unit, I could tell it would make for interesting content in the *Reader*. After all, no one knew of the unit's existence. So I told Bob Roth, the *Reader*'s publisher and my old boss, about it, and he agreed. He then got McClory to handle the reporting. (All the *Reader*'s writers were freelancers.)

As McClory noted, the program had been created eight years earlier by Democrat Edward Hanrahan, who was then the Cook County State's Attorney. It was designed to Roto-Rooter a docket clogged and overflowing with both righteous cases requiring prosecution and ridiculous cases that should never have been filed. How to ferret them out before they got that far was the question that needed answering.

Hanrahan's idea was to create a kind of task force of state's attorneys who would be dispatched to police stations around the city, where they could review the details of felonies that cops wanted to file, and either sign off on them or reject them. At any given time, there were about 27 attorneys working in Felony Review (out of 550 total ASAs), each of whom served about nine months or so before moving, typically, into a felony preliminary hearing court before becoming a felony trial assistant. The shifts were three days in a row, either from six in the morning to six at night or from six at night to six in the morning, followed by three days off, followed by three days in a row of the opposite shift.

Felony Review Headquarters were in the State's Attorney's offices at 26th and California in the new office tower next to the old Criminal Court Building. There were also branch offices in each of the six Chicago PD Area Headquarters; that's where much of the work was done because that's where the detectives were located. If a patrol officer made an arrest, it was the detective who had to sign off on seeking felony charges. If the detective sought charges, it was the Felony Review assistants who had to approve them before they could be filed. If disapproved, the police could still file a misdemeanor complaint.

If that happened, the Felony Review "reject" would show up on the docket of a misdemeanor branch court where some rookie ASA would need to handle it—possibly without realizing why it had been rejected by Felony Review. Was something missing? Was the credibility of the complainant in doubt? Or maybe there was an absence of key physical evidence. As I learned the hard way, assessing why this case hadn't passed muster was difficult for a relatively inexperienced misdemeanor prosecutor.

The Felony Review assistant's job was twofold: First, we had to sign off on search warrants before cops could take them to a judge for a signature. But our main function was to review felony charges and either approve or disapprove them after evaluating the case as it existed at that stage. That meant interviewing witnesses, gauging their credibility, checking the paperwork, talking with the cops, and, if possible, getting a statement from the suspect. In addition to screening out bad cases, our aim was to anticipate what a future felony trial assistant would want to have been done at the police station in order to help prove the case and/or anticipate and negate possible defense arguments.

To that end, even if we could not obtain a confession of guilt, we wanted to lock the accused into a story on the spot before they (or their lawyer) could devise a more credible one that better fit what they later learned was the evidence. In this way, even an "exculpatory" statement asserting innocence might be inculpatory at trial.

For example, suppose a defendant insisted that, while he was present at the scene of the crime, he had done nothing wrong and had nothing to do with whatever crime had taken place. While seemingly exculpatory, by placing himself at the scene, such a statement took witness misidentification off the table as a possible defense. Or if the accused provided us with an alibi we could later disprove, it would be difficult for the defendant to come up with a better one later on.

The only felonies that did not require Felony Review approval were drug crimes. Some believed the rationale for that exemption was to keep ASAs away from the corruption surrounding drug law enforcement. It may also have been that there would be little to "review" when cops were the only witnesses to what is literally a victimless crime. That's not a larger political point. What matters is there are no civilian witnesses whose credibility needs to be assessed. And an ASA would have little basis to question a cop's narrative of a drug bust. The confiscated drugs would speak for themselves.

"The ordinary police officer," Chuck Hartmann, the co-director of Felony Review, explained to McClory, "is thinking first about grabbing an offender, and he's concerned about his own arrest statistics and his promotion chances within the department. The investigator is thinking about nabbing the felon, too, but his big job is getting identification from the witnesses so a decision on charges can be made. Now, the Felony Review attorney is supposed to be thinking ahead as a prosecutor at trial. It's his job to evaluate the evidence and determine if the case can stand up in court whenever it comes up. That's a different perspective."

As for the effectiveness of Felony Review, the numbers didn't lie. In the previous year, the article noted, 13,200 felony cases had been filed in Cook County. But that number would've been more than 21,000 if Felony Review hadn't weeded out the ones that, for whatever reason, shouldn't have made it into the court system. As a result, the amount of time before cases were adjudicated or pleaded out had been significantly reduced. Even better, the vast majority of cases that were charged ended in guilty pleas or verdicts because the evidence was strong.

McClory introduced me in the story as a twenty-seven-year-old Harvard Law grad whose fellow Ivies couldn't believe he'd passed up Big Law for a chance to earn $17,000 a year as a county prosecutor. (My starting salary was actually $15,600.)

"I'm not the same lawyer I was before I got into this unit," I told him on the record. "When you see a case like we do at stage one, you gain an appreciation for anything that makes it all the way through to trial. You know, the case never gets better than when we first see it. In court, it only gets worse—with the lapse of time and failing memories." And of course, the case also gets worse when the prosecution is up against the skills of a clever defense attorney who knows how to win a case that isn't completely buttoned down (and even a case that is).

At the time I was assigned to Felony Review, I was not yet married and was living in Chicago. Sometimes, when getting off my twelve-hour shift, I'd drive to the townhome my parents had moved to in Orland Park, about twenty miles west of my boyhood home town of Calumet City. There, I'd spend my twelve hours off between shifts because it gave me a chance to see my folks.

When I worked the night shift, I'd get there after six in the morning, just about when my dad was getting up to go to work. By this time, he had closed his laundry on the South Side of Chicago and was doing well in the retail furniture business in Orland Park. Before he left for the store, he wanted to hear everything about the night I'd had on Felony Review.

"If you don't tell me now, you'll never remember to tell me later," he would say.

Typically, so much had happened in those twelve hours that it was hard to remember everything anyway, but he ate up anything I told him. The chapters that follow are based on transcripts of statements by defendants, a few police reports I happened to save, and one of my two Felony Review log books, in which we recorded every case we worked. These books also recorded my approval/disapproval statistics, which were calculated weekly by our staff and entered by them in our log books. I have also confirmed what details I could glean from various online sources, including press accounts, and from appellate court opinions.

Sadly, my other log book was lost somewhere along the line, during my moves from Chicago, to Evanston, to Boston, and to DC. So you can assume there were twice as many good stories as I can report here.

A Montage
"Is it Okay if we turn the body over?"

ONE HOMICIDE I worked took place on the North Side, literally across the street from the district police station to which I responded. A man had been arrested for stabbing his wife to death after an argument that was so loud the neighbors could hear the yelling. She had definitely been stabbed. And she was definitely dead. But was it murder?

The cops asked me if I wanted to view the scene, which was a 2nd-floor apartment in a three-story walk-up, not unlike my apartment building. There in the bedroom, on the floor next to the bed, was the body of the wife lying on her stomach. The apartment was jammed with uniformed officers and detectives. It was winter, and everyone was tracking snow from outside into the apartment. Not the immaculate crime scene one sees on TV.

I entered the room and looked at the body. This would be the only time I saw a corpse on the job. The detective who was down on one knee examining it looked up at me and asked, "Is it okay if we turn the body over?"

He was busting my balls. No way did this veteran detective need permission from a twenty-something lawyer. I played along.

"Sure," I said.

He rolled the body over, and the back of the corpse's hand landed kerplunk on the top of my leather boot.

I ended up rejecting murder charges for the husband. Why? First of all, I interviewed the husband, who described the argument he had with his wife. He told me that she had taken a kitchen knife off the counter and tried to stab him with it. After a struggle, he wrestled the knife away from her. He then left the apartment, and when he did so, she was alive and well—or so he claimed.

Naturally, I was skeptical of every aspect of this story, but my job was to corroborate or impeach it if I could. So I interviewed the neighbors who had heard the argument and reported it to the cops. They told me they could hear the door of the apartment slam as the husband left. Crucially, they also told me they could hear the wife still shouting after him after they heard the door slam. I asked if they were positive about this.

They were.

So she *was* still alive and (seemingly) well when he left, as her husband had claimed.

Then there was the physical evidence. The wife had only been stabbed once in the chest. The knife wound had penetrated the lung. It seemed apparent that—as later confirmed by the medical examiner—she was bleeding internally into her lungs without realizing it. Eventually, she felt ill and went to lie down, but lying down only accentuated the filling of her lungs. Perhaps hoping to get help she tried to walk from her bedroom before collapsing on the floor at the foot of the bed where I had seen her.

That single stab wound likely would have occurred during the struggle for the knife, and the husband would not even have known it had happened, as his wife continued to berate him when he left the apartment. In the heat of the argument and the fight for the knife, with her adrenaline flowing, even she might not have realized she had been stabbed. Or so a defense attorney would argue. And rightfully so.

So I let him go. *One* stab wound meant he was free to go. One stab wound made it an accident—indeed, self-inflicted—not a murder. But had there been *two* stab wounds, he would have been charged with murder.

An innocent man was saved from criminal prosecution that day without even the need to retain a lawyer. Felony Review did its job.

"You guard these guys"

I'D BEEN WORKING Area 1, located on South Wentworth Avenue on the near South Side of Chicago right next to the Dan Ryan Expressway and the Robert Taylor Homes, the Soviet-style high-rise project that has mercifully since been torn down. The station was a contemporary structure in the brutalist style, with those vertical slat windows, very thin, which gave off the air of a prison. Its huge radio tower announced its location from a mile away. While I was interviewing two suspects in one of the interview rooms, someone else in custody escaped.

That's when I learned that police departments go into a frenzy when something like this happens. In cop world, it's the equivalent of losing your weapon in the military, so everybody drops whatever they're doing and runs out of the building in a mass exodus to find the guy. I later witnessed the same thing happen at a North Side district police station.

Figure 21. Area 1 Headquarters at 51st and Wentworth

Before joining in the search, the detective working this interview with me said, "You guard these guys."

I figured, *Well, okay, I'll just leave them in the interview room by themselves. The door locks from the outside. I can read or something while I'm waiting for everyone to get back.* Which they did in about a half hour, having caught the escapee. When the detective returned, I asked him how the suspect had escaped custody. Answer: "They got out through a window in the interview rooms."

It seemed the architects designing the building had made the interview room windows operable from the inside.

"An interview room like this one?"

"Yeah. Same."

"Oh, shit."

We opened the door, and both men were still sitting there. I emitted the loudest silent *whew* ever uttered.

Did you look for the shotgun?

I WAS QUESTIONING a man named Kendrick Carroll about the murder of Robert Patterson. The court reporter was there, too, taking down everything about how Carroll and Patterson had gotten into a fistfight when Carroll refused to share his beer with Patterson.

"He said, 'Can I have some?,' and he grabbed the can, you know, and I grabbed it back and he hit me in the chest. We transferred punches. We got to arguing and stuff and transferred punches, you know."

Patterson got the better of the shoving match and had to be pulled off Carroll by others in the group. Carroll then left and retrieved a shotgun he had hidden in a plastic bag under some leaves against a nearby building.

About fifteen minutes later, Carroll returned to where Patterson and the group were hanging out. Patterson approached Carroll, and Carroll pulled the plastic bag off the shotgun. Patterson said, "Stop playing with me with that thing." As Patterson pushed the barrel of the gun away, he said, "Go ahead on." Carroll then held the gun "real tight so he would not take it from me." The gun was pointing at Patterson's stomach when Carroll pulled the trigger and blasted him with the 12 gauge.

"After you shot the gun, where did you go?" I asked Carroll.

"I ran and threw the gun away."

"Where did you throw the gun?"

"On the tracks . . ."

"Did anybody see you throw the gun up there?"

"It might have been three dudes seen me."

"The tracks" to which Carroll referred were the Chicago Transit Authority "elevated" train tracks that ran past the Robert Taylor Homes on a one-story high embankment. After throwing the gun away, Carroll ran to 47th and King Drive, caught a bus, and rode it all night.

"I didn't know what to do," he told me.

After interviewing Carroll, I asked the cops if they'd found the gun. They hadn't.

"Did you go up on the tracks and look for it?"

"No."

"Why not?"

"Because that gun wouldn't have even hit the ground before someone else snatched it up." Ergo, in the cops' opinion, there was no point in looking.

"You may be right," I said. "You probably are. But we've gotta go look for it because we—you, me—have to say we looked for it."

Their silence made me continue. "Look, if you're asked in court by the defense attorney, or the judge asks, you can't say you didn't look because you knew it wasn't going to be there. But if you go look for it and it's not there, you can truthfully say you looked."

As my job called for, I was anticipating what defense lawyers would do and trying to eliminate any winning points for the defense from the equation.

"Okay," the cops said. "But if we gotta go, then so do you."

I was telling them something they didn't want to hear, which meant I had to be punished, too. But I surprised them. "Yeah," I said enthusiastically, "come on, let's go."

We drove to where Carroll had told us he had ditched the gun and parked both cop cars next to the embankment. It was the middle of the night, but the street and tracks were illuminated by the orange vapor streetlights. To reach the tracks, we climbed onto the hood of the car, then onto the roof. As I lifted my leg from the roof of the car to launch myself up onto the embankment, I could feel my brown jeans ripping in the crotch, then splitting wide open at the seam.

The cops had been right: The shotgun couldn't be found. But at least they would be able to answer honestly about whether they'd looked for it.

Back at the station, I had to take Carroll's statement, keeping my legs crossed the whole time so Carroll, the court reporter, and the homicide investigator couldn't see my white Jockeys.

Begging for bologna

IT'S REFERRED TO as "the great Chicago blizzard of 1979." Between January 13 and 14, twenty-one inches fell, making this one of the worst blizzards in the city's history. All of northern Illinois and northwest Indiana were affected. Winds gusted to forty miles per hour, and by the second night, there were about thirty inches of snow pretty much everywhere in the city. Five people died, one of them when a snowplow driver lost control and smashed into thirty-four cars. O'Hare Airport was closed for four days. Getting things back to normal took forever. In fact, the city's horrible response under Mayor Michael Bilandic, who'd taken over after the death of Richard "Boss" Daley, was what would get Jane Byrne elected mayor the following year.

I'd been scheduled for a Felony Review shift the night of January 13 and was instructed, as all other Felony Review prosecutors were, to pack a bag, report to headquarters at 26th and Cal, and prepare to stay on shift until conditions cleared. We would be handling all the cases in the county by telephone, which is how we normally handled property crimes. Now even murders would be handled by phone.

Figure 22. Looking west on 53rd Street in Hyde Park, January 15, 1979

On a night like that, you would of course assume that there'd be little to no crime, and in fact that's what happened. The biggest problem we faced in the building was that there was also nothing to eat and no place open to buy anything. Word came down from the top authorizing us to break into—not pay for—any of the vending machines in the building. But a couple of us decided instead to bundle up and walk the few hundred feet that separated the criminal courthouse from the Cook County Jail.

My only previous time in the jail was to run a lineup, and I hadn't thought much about it before I got there. But when I was ushered into the area where prisoners were housed and the thick metal doors were shut behind me, I was filled with trepidation. The feeling only intensified as I was led down narrow corridors bisected by a yellow stripe, with lines of prisoners in their tan jumpsuits coming the other way in single file, keeping to their right. Same as I did walking in the opposite direction. With a guard just ahead and just behind me.

The architecture of the jail was neoclassical, like the courthouse. Its huge metal doors looked like something off a medieval castle. The doors were closed and locked, of course, so we pounded on them. At last, a jail guard came and opened them. We told him who we were, and he escorted us to the warden's office, where the warden and his staff were playing cards while music from a boom box filled the room.

Figure 23. Cook County Jail

They were only too happy to provide us with the famed "Cook County Jail bologna sandwiches." White bread, bologna, no mustard. The food that prisoners got when traveling to and from court.

We returned to our office and ate those bologna sandwiches in what turned out to be one of my favorite nights as a Felony Review prosecutor. And thanks to the snow, neither cops nor Felony Review lawyers had anything else to do that night.

Which reminds me of another quiet night I spent with a fellow Felony Review assistant. Like me, he was a big fan of the Hitchcock film, *North by Northwest*. I happened to have purchased a paperback containing the screenplay, and we took turns reading the lines to each other. I recall his favorite line was from the auction scene in which the auctioneer refers to "this lovely Aubusson settee." My favorite line was Cary Grant's Roger Thornhill reply to Eva Marie Saint's Eve Kendall, as they were kissing in her stateroom on the train from New York to Chicago, when she said: "You're very clever with words. You can probably make them do anything for you. Sell people things they don't need. Make women who don't know you fall in love with you." To this Thornhill replied, "I'm beginning to think I'm underpaid." My next favorite line was when Thornhill asked Eve Kendall, "Tell me. What do you do besides lure men to their doom on the Twentieth Century Limited?"

"I used a rubber"

IN THE MIDDLE of the night, I was dispatched from Area 2 Headquarters to a district police station on the far South Side. An older black man had been arrested for the rape of a younger black woman and was in custody. I was called to the station by the two Area 2 homicide-sex detectives to whom the case was assigned. After I arrived, I interviewed the woman as a complaining witness, then interviewed the arrestee.

One thing you learn early on in Felony Review that serves you well, not just during your time in Felony Review but also as a trial lawyer, is to stop trying to ascertain whether you believe people subjectively or disbelieve them subjectively. Good liars lie well, and good people often tell the truth badly. You can't go by your gut. As a Felony Review assistant, all your decisions should be made on the basis of the evidence, as if you were a magistrate or a judge. Is the evidence there? If so, proceed. But if you do proceed, what's a defense lawyer likely to make of this case?

In truth, more than justice was at stake. The job of a Felony Review lawyer was to pass cases on to felony trial assistants who were senior to us. Depending on what we handed them to prosecute and the disposition of the cases, our reputations in the State's Attorney's Office would be affected, and our performance would help determine what kinds of posts we got down the line after our Felony Review missions ended. If we gave them garbage cases with no chance or little chance of a guilty verdict, we'd be tagged as know-nothings unfit to climb in the hierarchy. I knew Felony Review lawyers who'd gotten calls from felony assistants at 26th Street asking how the hell some "horseshit" case ever got approved. No one wanted to get a call like that.

Which was exactly why I learned to never trust my gut. I trusted only the facts and evidence.

Well, maybe not never. This case was one of the exceptions.

"She's a prostitute," the arrestee said. "I picked her up. We did it. And I didn't pay her. That's what this is about. I swear, that's what this was about."

How do you prove a negative like that? Even for prostitutes with long rap sheets, the laws against rape aren't suspended.

Then he blurted out, "I used a rubber."

His hands shaking, he reached back for his wallet and pulled out another wrapped condom as proof. Rapists rarely use rubbers.

Was that dispositive evidence that it had been a consensual, if unpaid, encounter? Of course not. But the gestalt of the situation—the condom, his shaking hand, the tone in his voice, the look on his face, the fear in his eyes, his lack of a record for anything remotely like this—all of it together made me believe him. So, largely on the basis of a gut feeling—and the fact that this was a he-said, she-said situation—I let him go. Making sure they were out of earshot of the arresting tactical officers, the detectives quietly told me they concurred.

In Chicago, tactical or "tac" officers are sometimes called "headhunters" because they're out to make arrests, not collect evidence to establish guilt beyond a reasonable doubt. Tactical teams operate in high-crime areas, focusing on street-level crime enforcement. Unlike patrolmen, tac officers worked in plain clothes, but they were not detectives. Detectives *investigate*. (Indeed, in Chicago, detectives were formally called "investigators.")

Like Felony Review assistants, detectives stay behind their desks until after an arrest is made—much as they were depicted in *NYPD Blue*. Tactical officers *arrest*. They were the cops who picked this guy up and would get credit for the arrest if he were charged. In contrast, detectives get credit for "clearing" a case, whether by bringing charges or by classifying a case as "unfounded."

If you are old enough to remember *Hill Street Blues*, Dennis Franz's ill-fated character, Sal Benedetto (who appeared during the show's 3rd season), captured the spirit of a tactical officer, complete with leather sports coat. Although billed on the series as a "detective" from the vice squad, Benedetto's character was more like the aggressive plain clothes tac officers who patrolled the streets in unmarked cars and converged on crimes in progress. (I am not suggesting that tac officers were corrupt, as Benedetto turned out to be—though corrupt vice cops were a dime a dozen. That's where the money is.)

I left the suspect sitting in the cell while I went out and told the tac officers that I would not be approving charges. They were pissed and argued with me pretty heatedly. Who knows? Maybe they were right. But my judgment was bolstered by the fact that the detectives concurred with me on this. Indeed, this was probably why they called me to the station in the first place. In the face of the tac officers, they wanted the decision to come from a state's attorney, not from them.

It was now about three in the morning. I had some paperwork I needed to fill out to dispose of this thing, which I did in the vacant day room where the street cops have their desks for roll call. The detectives were just hanging around nearby, but I thought little of that until I got up to leave the station. As I did, the two detectives walked out with me and escorted me to my squad car.

It now became clear to me that they had loitered as they did to protect me from the tac officers, who were pretty hot about my decision. What exactly did the detectives fear would happen? Would the tac officers have come at me physically? Probably not. Would they have tried to hector and intimidate me into changing my mind into referring the case for prosecution? Definitely. Would I have yielded to them? No. I was still that kid from Cal City and Ron Barnett's son. But these detectives didn't know that. They were just making sure I wouldn't be intimidated, physically or verbally. I always appreciated that.

The hogs did it

AT ABOUT 4:45 in the morning, the body of Robert Robinson, age forty, was found in a hog pen in the American Meat Packing Company. He was dead and naked. Robinson, who worked as a security guard for the Wackenhut Security Company, was last seen the day before when he reported for work.

After the company was able to remove the 105 hogs, each weighing about three hundred pounds, from the pen, the police were able to examine the body. His head was half eaten away, along with his entire crotch and part of his stomach. The body was taken to the morgue to be examined by the medical examiner. The cause of death was listed as natural causes, noting that the victim had coronary artery disease. But why was the deceased naked? How could we be sure there was no foul play? (These being hogs, we were at least certain there was no *fowl* play.)

The responding homicide investigators noted a key fact in their report: "The victim's clothes, a blue set of pants and shirt, and also his undershorts were hung up outside the pen on a pole. The pants and shirt were uniform security clothes of the Wackenhut Corp. The victim's hat was found under the north rail of the hog pen."

What the investigators told me, but did not include in their report, was their conclusion that the deceased had stripped naked to have sex with one of the hogs. At some point, either because the hogs objected or because he had a heart attack, the victim fell to the ground, where the hogs then proceeded to do what hogs do when presented with a food source.

Cops and lawyers tell lots of "war stories" that one needs to take with a grain of salt. Not this one. It was entirely unseasoned. (And I saved the police report in case anyone questioned my veracity.)

* * *

These were the kinds of stories my dad made me stay up after my shift to tell him before he went to work and I went to sleep. And he was right. I have indeed forgotten more of these stories than I remember.

There were, however, two stories involving murder confessions that I will never forget. One case stands out for what I did right. But the first story is about how I nearly blew it.

"Did I Give This Guy His *Miranda* Rights?"

CESAR MARIN WAS accused of murdering a Korean liquor store owner named Ryok Kim and critically wounding his wife, Ihn Kang Kim, shooting them both in a holdup.

The liquor store was a big move for the couple, who had come to the United States from Korea six years earlier. They'd scratched together their savings from their small knick-knack shop on the South Side to buy the liquor store on the North Side where they could live in an apartment upstairs while they kept long hours with no help. When they wrote home excitedly to Korea about it, they said it was a good place to have a business. A safe place, too.

Cesar Marin was an immigrant from Colombia who had lived in Chicago for the past two years. The Kims' liquor store was on the corner of North Broadway and Bryn Mawr Avenue in the Edgewater neighborhood, just three short blocks from Marin's apartment (and about three miles from mine).

On March 24, Marin had been drinking all day, from 3:30 in the afternoon to midnight, consuming two six-packs of Old Style beer and a pint of Seagram's. Bored of watching TV and with nothing else to do, he decided to head to Lake Michigan, about a ten-minute walk from his apartment. Before leaving, he put a pistol in the front waistband of his pants and a knife into the right front pocket of his jacket. He also took along another pint of Seagram's, which he drank at the lake, sitting by himself.

As he passed the Kims' liquor store on his way home, he decided to stop and buy more beer for later. Back before the Kims owned it, he had worked in that store for about a week before taking a job at the Warner Candy Company in the Ravenswood neighborhood, so he knew its layout, including the basement, where the cleaning equipment and garbage were kept.

Marin took a six-pack of Old Style from the refrigerator case and put it on the counter. Mr. Kim asked him for $2.25, which he paid. Then Marin noticed that Mr. Kim was starting to close up the store by turning off some of the lights. That was when Marin produced his pistol and told Kim that he didn't want to pay for the beers. Holding the gun on them, he directed Kim and his wife to go down into the basement.

When they got downstairs, Marin told Mr. Kim to give him his money. Kim gave him about $250 in bills he had in his pocket and told him, "You got the money, okay. Go home."

As Marin went to leave, he sensed that Mr. Kim was making a move toward him, so he opened fire. Whether it was to aid her husband or resist Marin, Mrs. Kim then moved in Marin's direction, and he opened fire on her, too. He stopped firing when he saw Mr. Kim collapse to the floor. While lying on the floor, Mr. Kim grabbed Marin's leg. Marin pulled out his knife and stabbed Kim two or three times, then began stabbing Mrs. Kim.

They were moaning and bleeding on the floor as he went up the stairs, where he found a two-by-four and nailed it to the basement door, preventing the Kims from opening it and reaching the telephone. Leaving the beer behind, he returned to his apartment, where he had a few more drinks before falling asleep.

Ihn could hear her husband lying next to her gasping, barely alive. She reached out to cover his wounds and stop his bleeding. "Must we die like this?" she asked him. "Must our dream end like this, in ashes?" She resolved to herself, *I will not let that happen.*

In a moving column, Anne Keegan of the *Chicago Tribune* described what happened next: Shot in the stomach and stabbed, Mrs. Kim

> staggered to her feet, and in the dark dampness she groped for the light chain and pulled it. Her husband lay near her on the floor. Hysterical, she crawled up the basement stairs and pounded futilely on the door. There was no answer, no sound at all except the whirr of the refrigeration unit as its motor kicked on and off. She pounded and pounded, but no one heard. It was Sunday morning, and no one would come looking for them until later that day.
>
> Ihn began to claw at the head of the stairs. Her fingernails ripped at the wall. A piece of plaster fell. She began to pound and dig and scratch. More plaster fell. With her two small hands she tore at the wall, pulling out the plaster in chunks and ripping away

> the lathing. She kept it up until she could reach her hand through a hole to the bottles of liquor in the shelves on the other side. …
>
> She banged and ripped at the wall until she'd ripped out a 12- by 9-inch hole. Two wooden joists prevented her from ripping it any wider. [She put her head through the small hole and painfully squeezed her body through the small opening,] knocking over the liquor bottles as she worked her way over them and out into the store. Her wounds were bleeding. Her hands were raw. When she finally made it, she pulled herself up and staggered, exhausted, out onto the street.

Mrs. Kim told Keegan: "I got outside and asked for help. Nobody stopped for me. Finally, I forced someone to stop and I told them my story. I told them my husband was in the basement and they took him out. 'Please go see my husband. Do not worry about me.'"

After the attack, until he was arrested, Marin could not sleep well. When he tried to sleep, he kept picturing the man he had left bleeding on the basement floor. Mr. Kim died of his wounds in the basement, but his wife survived and told the police that her assailant's name was "Cesar."

Four days later, I was sitting in my office at Area 6 homicide at Belmont and Western, the same place where I had taken the confession of Juan Caballero. At around 10:00 p.m., Sergeant Edward Flynn of Area 6 homicide contacted me, and I walked over to the offices of the Homicide-Sex Unit. I'd worked with him before and found him to be a conscientious cop. After briefing me on the Kims' case, he told me they had arrested a man named Cesar who fit the description of the assailant.

Flynn asked me to approve homicide charges against the arrestee for the murder of Ryok Kim. But as a Felony Review assistant, we could only approve homicide charges in consultation with one of our two supervisors, either Charles "Chuck" Hartmann or Sander "Sandy" Clapman. (Both are pictured in the *Reader* cover story that appears above.) On this night, Chuck Hartmann was on duty.

Although Mrs. Kim was in Edgewater Hospital in critical condition,

Hartmann told me we needed to get her to ID the perpetrator from a set of photographs of different persons. This is called a "photo ID." Flynn protested that it was not necessary and that Mrs. Kim wasn't up to it, but Hartmann called the shots. So I went with Flynn to the hospital. To everyone's amazement, when I showed her the photos, she told me the person we had in custody was not their assailant. And she was adamant about it.

The cops had arrested the wrong Cesar.

Not long thereafter, the police located and arrested another Cesar: Cesar Marin. This Cesar was caught with proceeds from the crime and the murder weapon, so the cops were sure they had the right man. They did not see the need for another photo identification. But this time it was I who insisted.

I returned to the hospital with six photos of men who looked reasonably similar to Marin, plus an image of Marin himself. It was heartrending to see her lying there, tubes coming out of her, including a drain from her nose. Her hand trembled as she took each photo and studied it. I will never forget how the sight of Marin's face in the picture disturbed her so utterly and instantly that the fluids began to pour through the tube in her nose as she repeatedly poked the photograph with her outstretched index finger.

A year later, Ihn told *Chicago Tribune* columnist Anne Keegan that she was in shock for weeks. She would not talk or move her eyes or respond to others. She did not know her husband was dead. "She does not remember much, she says, of that month and a half in the hospital." But she was clear-headed enough four days after the attack to clear an innocent man who had been arrested and to literally finger the man who murdered her husband. Thanks also to Felony Review.

It was a very strong case. We had a suspect who'd been caught with the booty. We had an excellent, compelling eyewitness. We even had the gun. What remained was to see if we could get him to confess.

Our normal procedure was for the Felony Review assistant to try to question the person that the police considered to be a suspect, obtaining a statement whenever possible. Back then, there were no audio- or video-recorded confessions. Should that person confess verbally to the state's attorney, one of our court reporters would be dispatched to the station so the statement could be given a second time: The court reporter would then transcribe and type it up, and the accused would sign it. We would have the accused read every page of his confession and initial it. Going from oral questioning to signed confession is not a short process. I worked from 10:00 p.m. to 5:00 a.m. the next morning on this case—but this approach yielded an excellent conviction rate.

Cesar Marin spoke excellent English. But just as I'd worried about the defense attorney asking if the cops had looked for the missing weapon, I could foresee counsel making the argument that this immigrant from Colombia hadn't actually confessed because his English was so poor. So, they would argue, the confession was obviously a fiction created by the cops and the prosecutor. How to negate that argument?

As fate would have it, that night I was training a young attorney named Jimmy Linn, who had recently been transferred to Felony Review. I explained to Jimmy that, to guard against this future line of attack, I would ask the detectives to find a bilingual cop and have him brought into the interrogation room, in which the confession would be given in the presence of a court reporter, who'd take down every word. That's what we did. Present for his statement were the investigating detective, the court reporter, a bilingual officer, and Jimmy.

I began the court-ordered statement: "The record should reflect that it is the 28th of March, 1979, at approximately 1:45 a.m.; and we are in Area 6 in an interview room. Present with me is Sergeant Edward Flynn of the Chicago Police Department Homicide-Sex Unit; Steve Barrientos, of the Chicago Police Department; Assistant State's Attorney Jimmy Linn; court reporter Emmett Smith, and Mr. Cesar Marin.

"The record should reflect that Officer Barrientos is a fluent speaker of Spanish and that he assisted us in speaking earlier this evening with Mr. Marin and that although Mr. Marin does speak English, he does have some difficulty at times. Now Cesar, I want to tell you that I am going to ask you some questions about what happened within the last week, and if at any time you don't understand my questions or in some way are unable to answer my questions, in English the way you like, you should feel free to ask Officer Barrientos for translation. Do you understand that?"

"Yes," Marin replied.

"Is that the way we did it earlier this evening?"

"Yes."

I then proceeded to question Cesar Marin, who provided all the details about his actions and the murder that I described above. His confession was long and detailed, right down to how many bullets had been fired and from where. He was completely relaxed throughout.

The nice thing about court transcripts is that they elide pauses. Whether they're two seconds or two minutes, they do not show up in the transcript. When I reached the end of a confession, I would always sit quietly for a minute or two thinking about whether I'd forgotten anything. This time, a thought stunningly occurred to me:

Wait a second. Did I give this guy his Miranda *rights?*

I leaned over and whispered into Jimmy's ear low enough that no one else could hear, "Did I Mirandize him?"

"I think so," he whispered back.

Which isn't the same as "Yeah, absolutely," so I asked Sergeant Flynn, who actually said, "Yeah, absolutely." Even so, I still wasn't convinced. The only person now who would know for sure was the court reporter.

"Emmett," I said, "can you go back and check whether I gave Mr. Marin his *Miranda* rights?" He said he was sure I had but he would be happy to check.

Going all the way back to the beginning of the paper tape with his shorthand typing on it, he said, "Well, no, you didn't."

Instantly, I knew why I hadn't. Admonishing the suspect on the availability of an interpreter had thrown me off my normal protocol. I had advised Marin about the Spanish-speaking cop, but not about his right to remain silent.

Here I was, making sure all the details were just right as I trained another state's attorney to do this job, giving him a splendid tutorial in how not to fuck up a perfect case, and I had committed an unheard-of blunder. Now what? I was momentarily at a loss.

Then Jimmy leaned in and whispered in my ear, "Here's what to do. Before you took the oral confession from him, you gave him his *Miranda* rights, right? All you have to do is get him to reaffirm for the court reporter what you'd already done and the rights he'd already agreed to waive."

Right. Right, right, and right.

"Cesar," I then said, "do you remember earlier this evening I asked you to read the thing that was posted on the wall here in this room?"

"Yes."

"That was the statement of your rights?"

"Yes."

"That statement is in Spanish?"

"Yes."

"Did you read that statement?"

"Yes."

"After you read that statement, did I tell you again what your rights were? Did I read you your constitutional rights again?"

"Yes, you did."

"Did I have the policeman help explain those rights to you in Spanish?"

"Yes."

"The sergeant, who is also in this room, also advised you of your constitutional rights earlier this evening before you met me and he explained them to you?"

"Yes."

At this point, I pivoted to retroactively reading him his rights again.

"Did I tell you that you had a right to remain silent?"

"Yes."

"Did I tell you that anything you say can and will be used against you in a court of law?"

"Yes."

"Did I tell you that you have a right to a lawyer and have him present with you while you are being questioned?"

"Yes."

"Did I tell you that if you cannot afford to hire a lawyer, one can be appointed for you by the court to represent you at no cost to you before any questioning?"

"Yes."

"Did you understand all these rights when I told them to you before?"

"Yes."

"Do you understand all these rights now?"

"Yes."

"It was after understanding all these rights, after I told you these rights, that you spoke to me earlier this evening, is that right?"

"Yes."

"And you still understood all these rights when we spoke this time when the court reporter came in, is that right?"

"Yes."

"So this statement that you have just made to us in the presence of the court reporter was made with your understanding of all your rights, as I explained them to you before, is that right?"

"Yes."

After then asking him how long he had been in the country and speaking English and how well he had been treated by the police, I concluded the interview at 2:15 a.m., some forty-five minutes after it had begun. We waited until Emmett Smith had typed up the transcript of the interview. Officer Barrientos and I sat with Cesar as he initialed every page and printed his name at the end. He also made two minor corrections to the transcript, which is always a good thing because it indicates to a judge or jury that he really did read and understand the statement.

No one else in that room—not the cops, not the court reporter, not Jimmy Linn—had noticed that I hadn't gotten his *Miranda* on the written record. But thanks to quick thinking by Jimmy, we salvaged the case by getting it on the record retroactively, and as a result the defense did not even file a motion to suppress. Marin was convicted of murder and went to prison for a very long time.

Ihn Kim recovered from her wounds and reopened the liquor store that had been hers and her husband's dream. She had to learn better English so she could deal with all the customers and suppliers. A year later, she told Anne Keegan, "I carry my husband with me while I work. In beginning, it was hard. I was crying inside. But I sing songs every morning to myself. … [O]ne is a Korean hymn that says, 'Soon the dark of night will come. While there is still light, don't waste time—work hard and good things will come.' That makes me strong and I say, 'All right. I'm young: I'm in America.' And I'm on my way, and I get back to work."

Ihn filled the liquor store with plants and flowers. "I grow with them," she told Keegan with a smile. "Every day, like them, I grow stronger. I am like this flower, for I too am going to bloom in America."

I sincerely hope she did.

As for Jimmy Linn, he would go on to become an associate Cook County Circuit Court judge. In 2004, then-Chicago resident Oprah Winfrey tried to beg off jury duty in the murder trial of Dion Coleman. Both lawyers for the prosecution and defense told Judge Linn that they thought the talk show host would be a distraction, but neither side would use one of its preemptory challenges to exclude her.

Linn refused to remove her "for cause." "I'm not going to say that somebody is too important in our society to be a member of a jury," he told the lawyers. "I have no concern at all that the stars of this trial are going to be the trial lawyers, and the overriding personalities are going to be the lawyers and, to some extent, even the court." Oprah ended up voting to convict Coleman, whom Linn later sentenced to forty-five years in prison.

And that was not the last time Jimmy Linn was involved in a heater case featuring a celebrity. In 2022, he took some flak for his sentencing of Jussie Smollett after a jury found Smollett guilty of a class 4 felony for making a false report of a hate crime—falsely claiming that he was accosted by two Trump supporters. Linn sentenced Smollett to 150 days in jail. He had stepped up to hear the case after two other judges were "ill" the day the case was assigned.

Jimmy Linn was, and remains, the smart, stand-up, principled lawyer who saved my bacon.

"I'd Kill Michael For Sure"

EARLIER, I TOLD the story of the grisly murder of three young men—Michael Salcido, seventeen, his brother Arthur, nineteen, and their friend Frank Mussa, sixteen—who'd driven from Princeton, Illinois, about a hundred miles southwest of Chicago, and tried to buy marijuana from members of the Latin Kings street gang at the King Kastle hamburger stand. The gang members were Luis Ruiz, Juan Caballero, Placido LaBoy, and Nelson Aviles.

As I had with Cesar Marin, I spent many hours with Juan Caballero, one of the four gang members, and the only one who was willing to make a statement for the court reporter. LaBoy and Aviles refused to talk to the cops or to me. So, after a while, there was no way to hold them, and they were released. (Sometime later, they were rearrested after more evidence was found.)

In my first face-to-face with Ruiz, he admitted his complicity. I asked him if he would be willing to give a statement to a court reporter. He said he would. I began to explain the procedure involved, and he replied that he had confessed to another murder, which he beat. So he knew all about the procedure. Ruiz was referring to the murder charge of which he'd been acquitted by Judge Eugene Pincham. Later on, after Juan gave his statement, I returned to show Luis some pictures of the victims. After viewing them, he said he would not give a court reporter's statement.

But it was my encounter with Juan Caballero that I most remember. Here was this clean-cut, handsome young man of nineteen who was so respectful that our exchanges might have been mistaken for those at a student-teacher conference. In this job, you met the lowest of the low who looked and acted the part as though they were from central casting. But you also met people like Juan, whose personality was in no way congruent with the deed he was alleged to have taken part in. Or, for that matter, congruent with the kind of guys he was hanging with.

The more time you spend with someone like this, the more of a rapport you build up, and the more details they offer, as if they're telling a friend or confidant a story that they'd find fascinating. Like sitting around a campfire. Or a dorm room. The initial confession went on for an hour or so. When he'd finished, I asked him whether he'd let me bring in a court reporter and do it all over again, for the record. If he had said no, I'd have had to use my notes and testify about them at his trial, as I would have to do with Luis Ruiz.

But he said yes. I called for the court reporter. It took him probably an hour to get there. In the interim, I continued to spend time with Caballero so he wouldn't get cold feet. We started again with the reporter, and for the record, I again gave him his *Miranda* rights and established that he understood them and accepted the terms.

As I went through all the same questions, he sometimes looked at me as if to see whether his answers had been satisfactory. He seemed to want my approval. My tone was soft and understanding, even as he recited the grisly details of the slaughter.

At the end of the statement, the court reporter had to go out and type up the conversation from his shorthand notes so Caballero could read it and initial each page. As he did so, I sat next to him while he carefully read and then initialed each page. He then signed the last page. Done. Over.

But as I've explained, my job as a Felony Review assistant was to anticipate anything that might short-circuit the prosecution down the line. What would a future prosecutor wish I had done in the police station while speaking directly to the murderer? With Cesar Marin, I anticipated the issue would be language—negating any suggestion that the full confession was fabricated because the defendant did not speak English. With Juan Caballero, what could it be? I thought I knew.

Here was this clean-cut, articulate, soft-spoken, handsome young man of nineteen with only a minimal criminal record. I could imagine the defense presenting him as a naive wannabe who'd gotten swept up in the events, didn't know how to get out of the position he was in without possibly getting killed himself, and standing by helplessly as the situation spiraled out of control with others as the prime movers. How could I head off any such defense?

I decided to ask him a question I wouldn't have asked if I didn't already have the whole confession signed and sealed.

"Juan, let me ask you," I said. "If you had it to do all over again, would you?"

The purpose of the question? It wasn't curiosity, per se. It was his state of mind.

He thought for a second and said, "If it was a sure thing."

I replied, "There is no such thing as a sure thing. You got caught."

"Really?" he said. "Well, a lot of Kings kill people without getting caught."

"Well, you got caught, Juan," I replied. "Would you do it if you had to do it all over again?"

His eyes moved about the way you do when you're thinking something in the abstract before answering:

"I'd kill Michael for sure, but I don't know about the other two."

Now I had him. Even though it wasn't recorded by the court reporter, I wrote up his response as a memo and appended it to the file. In court, it would be admissible as an oral statement that I could testify to.

* * *

A year later, I testified at Caballero's trial about his statements to me. His court-appointed attorney was Terry Ekl, whom I'd known since I clerked for Steve Connolly and Bill Dwyer (with whom he'd started a law practice). Terry, you will recall, had written a glowing recommendation in favor of my being hired as an assistant state's attorney. As Terry cross-examined me, I directed all my answers to the jury. I even turned their way; as if I were giving a closing argument. As I related the line, "I'd kill Michael for sure, but I don't know about the other two," I could see it affected them. Notwithstanding his youth and lack of much criminal record, they voted quickly to convict and then for the death penalty.

What I testified to turned out to be critically important when he appealed his death sentence, claiming it was overly harsh for the crimes he'd admitted to and been convicted of committing. The Illinois Supreme Court cited my testimony in denying his claim that the punishment didn't fit the crime and asserting that he'd in fact acted in a depraved manner:

> In this case defendant exhibited no remorse. After giving a statement, the assistant State's Attorney asked him if he had to do it over "would he do it again." Defendant stated that he would "if it was a sure thing." The assistant State's Attorney then said

> "there is no such thing as a sure thing. You got caught." Defendant replied "a lot of Kings kill people without getting caught." The assistant State's Attorney again replied: "Well, you got caught, Juan. Would you do it if you had to do it all over again." The defendant replied: "I'd kill Michael for sure, but I don't know about the other two."

Juan Caballero was not executed by the State of Illinois. In 1999, George Ryan, the Republican governor of Illinois, who was later indicted for corruption, declared a moratorium on death sentences being carried out, then commuted 160 sentences, including Caballero's. Also commuted was the sentence of Henry Brisbon, the I-57 murderer with an unquenchable thirst to kill. These two murderers could not have been more different from each other.

Why Criminals Confess to the Police

A LOT OF people wonder why anyone would confess to the police. Because doing so seems so contrary to self-interest, they assume the confession must have been coerced in some way by the cops. But while coerced confessions have surely happened in the United States in general and in Chicago in particular, by the time I reached the criminal justice system, I saw little evidence of such police practices. I always asked each suspect how well they were treated by the police before I arrived on the scene. In only one instance did a suspect inform me that he had been abused.

This is not to say that everyone else had been well treated. No doubt, it was hard for suspects to distinguish me from the cops. This is why I told every suspect I interviewed that I was a lawyer, though I also made it clear that I was not their lawyer and that I worked with the police. So it's quite possible that suspects did not inform me of abuse because they figured I was just another cop.

But surely, if this had been like the bad old days of hitting suspects in the head with a phone book or rubber hose, I would have gotten more of a sense that this was happening than I did.

This improvement in police behavior can probably be attributed to the Warren Court's decisions affirming the rights of the accused. Among the most important was to require *Miranda* warnings, named after the 1966 case, *Miranda v. Arizona*—the decision written by Chief Justice Earl Warren, the vote being not 9–0 but 5–4.

As that 5–4 margin suggests, the decision was then, and remains today, highly contested as outside the proper scope of the judiciary, with critics arguing it should not be extrapolated from the original meaning of the 4th and 5th Amendments. I am, however, not convinced by the criticisms.

While the original meaning of the text of the 4th and 5th Amendments does not specify any such judicial enforcement, modern originalism distinguishes between two distinct judicial activities. The first is the activity of interpretation—that is, identifying the original communicative content of the text. Is the information conveyed by the words on the page in context? Yes or no.

The second is the activity of giving legal effect to the original meaning of the text by means of judicial doctrines or rules—a.k.a. "constitutional law."

Such doctrines, of which there are countless numbers, are almost never in the text of the Constitution. That's because they are the means by which the text is applied to particular cases and controversies. To be sure, such doctrines should be "faithful" to the original meaning of the text, which is more than being merely consistent with that meaning. They should also be consistent with the original object, purpose, or functions of the text—the problems the text was adopted to solve.

But the lesson of this brief digression into constitutional theory is that "just where does it say that in the text?" is a far less persuasive objection to a judicial doctrine than many on both the right and left assume. Why? Because virtually none of constitutional law can be found in the text itself. The question is whether these doctrines serve the original functions of the text. That is the standard by which to assess the merits of the requirement that suspects be given their *Miranda* warnings.

From what I observed, having to assiduously adhere to *Miranda* warnings (or risk having the defendant cut loose) had an interesting effect on most cops. It made them far more cognizant of suspects' rights and gave them tacit ammunition to resist the entreaties of bad cops who might've wanted to violate those rights. Meanwhile, the effect on arrestees who'd been on the inside before, after having spoken to the police when arrested previously, was to make them more likely to shut up. No wonder. They'd had years behind bars to assess their mistake and vow to never again talk to the cops.

Most interesting were the suspects who'd just turned eighteen and were now subject to being tried as adults. These guys often spoke freely because, in general, the juvenile justice system encourages offenders to talk to the authorities. Frequently, those who do talk and come clean are let go. Then, when they pass the magic age of eighteen, they are suddenly shocked to discover that their sincere confessions after being apprised of their *Miranda* rights do not result in their release—at which point they fall into the cohort of regretters.

This is what happened after I explained *Miranda* rights to Eric Stanley and he continued to confess anyway:

"You're not doing this because of any threats or coercion?" I asked.

"No, sir."

"Nobody has coerced you in any way?"

"No, sir."

"Has anybody made any promises to you?"

"No, sir. But I want to ask a question. Will I be cut loose tonight?"

Pause.

"There's no way that we can tell you whether you are going to get cut loose, okay, I told you that before, didn't I?"

"Yes, sir."

I had asked him whether anybody had made any promises to him because law enforcement is not supposed to offer any such inducement to confess. Doing so makes it difficult to assess whether the confession is being made freely and honestly, or whether the suspect is telling the cops what they want to hear in return for some benefit, which renders the confession fundamentally unreliable.

One of my tactics as a Felony Review assistant was to convince a suspect to speak with me by promising to accurately record whatever they told me so it would be part of the file. This was, I said, their chance to get their side of the events on the record. But in one early interview of a suspect, I crossed the line by suggesting that he might benefit somehow from telling me what happened. I don't recall exactly what I told him, but by the time he "confessed," I'd begun wishing I hadn't said whatever it was I'd said. I realized I couldn't be sure whether he'd told me what he thought I wanted to hear, not what had really happened. Then and there, I vowed I would never make that mistake again. As a Felony Review assistant, I was not there to get convictions. I was there to ensure that justice was done for the guilty and innocent alike. *Especially* the innocent.

Which returns us to the question: Why would anyone "confess" to the cops unless they had either been coerced or improperly promised a benefit for doing so? During my time on Felony Review, I encountered pretty much all the reasons why arrestees talk to the police and then confess.

The most obvious and most common reason they talk is that they don't think they are confessing. They think they're talking themselves out of trouble. *Yeah, I was there, but I didn't do anything.* Well, that's not going to get you out of trouble. You've just eliminated identification as an issue, which is a big deal because now the cops and prosecutors don't have to worry about eyewitnesses or fingerprints. You've just told us you were there. Great. At a minimum, you've helped establish felony murder, which is or can be charged if a death results from the commission of a crime—even the death of a co-offender at the hands of the police. Anyone who participates in a crime that results in the death of someone—even a fellow perpetrator—can be held responsible for murder. So thanks.

Yes, I took part in the robbery, but I didn't shoot anyone. If true, that fact has no effect on a criminal's accountability for the acts of someone else with whom he was committing the crime. Hello again, felony murder.

A second reason criminals talk is guilt. They feel guilty about what they did, and confession, as in the Catholic Church, makes them feel better, as if expiating a sin. I think that motive applied to Cesar Marin, who murdered Ryok Kim, the liquor store owner. Marin's friend Henry had told me that Marin had been acting very nervously the next day and the day after.

When I asked Marin whether what Henry had told me was so, he replied, "Yes. I can't sleep after Monday."

When I asked him whether "that was because you were afraid of getting caught?" he replied, "Not for the police. No. For the man [Mr. Kim]. I don't know. I can't sleep. I go to my bed and I remember the guy on the floor and I can't sleep."

I then asked Marin, "You know what you did was wrong, don't you?"

To which he replied simply, "Yes."

Marin seemed genuinely contrite about what he'd done and was looking for a kind of absolution. I believed him. Not that it made any difference to me, and I of course offered him no absolution, which wasn't mine to offer anyway.

The third major reason I encountered for confessing was pride. Some of these guys were actually proud of what they'd done. Or, closely related, denying what they'd done would have been a cowardly lack of machismo. I think this is what motivated Juan Caballero to talk so openly with me about his heinous acts. He thought he had done the right thing and it would have been unmanly to deny it.

In his world—the world of one gang being mortal enemies of another gang whose ethnicity and social status are identical to theirs—the crime he'd taken part in was moral and justified. Given the offense against his gang that Michael had bragged about unwittingly—despite its being fabulist bluster—triple homicide was warranted. This is why when I asked him if he would do it again if he had the chance, he calmly, sincerely, and chillingly said, "I'd have killed Michael for sure, but I don't know about the other two."

* * *

After nine months, my time as a Felony Review assistant came to a close. Although I joined the State's Attorney's Office to learn to be a trial lawyer like on TV, my tenure on Felony Review was the most memorable experience I had as a prosecutor. It put me, a young Harvard Law grad, in police stations in the middle of the night, dealing with good and bad cops, victims, witnesses, and hardened criminals like Henry Brisbon and outwardly clean-cut killers like Juan Caballero.

Of course, the time spent on Felony Review was an important part of my training to be a felony trial prosecutor. It taught me what a case looked like before there were charges—or what it was supposed to look like. It helped me to distinguish between bullshit and legitimate cases.

But it was also an end in itself. It vindicated the reason I chose prosecution over defense: to see that justice was done on behalf of the guilty and innocent alike. I can state absolutely that in my time on Felony Review, we did a lot of good.

Drug Court

MY FIRST ASSIGNMENT after nine months on Felony Review was to Branch 42, the felony preliminary hearing court located at Belmont and Western in the building that also housed Area 6 Police Headquarters. That's where Jack Reynolds now presided as judge with Tommy Del Beccaro as his bond-slip hallway lawyer-fixer. Sometime after I left this assignment, and unknown to me at the time, my former ASA colleague Matt partnered with Del Beccaro as a case-fixer.

From there, I moved to Branch 25, one of the two narcotics courts, called "drug courts," that handled Chicago's drug cases. The other drug court was Branch 57. Branch 25 handled the larger cases. Their courtrooms were located next to each other at 26th and Cal, and it felt good to be back. But I was a bit squeamish about this particular assignment.

You see, I became a state court prosecutor, as opposed to a federal prosecutor, to prosecute real crimes like murder, rape, and armed robbery. As a libertarian, I thought—and still believe—that drug crimes are not real crimes and that it was unjust to imprison anyone for such an offense. What would I do now that I was being assigned to drug court?

At the time, my boss, Bernard Carey, the elected Republican State's Attorney of Cook County, favored diversion for marijuana and other small drug offenses. If a misdemeanor was involved, my job as a prosecutor in drug court was to divert those cases, which would eventually result in a dismissal. If it was a felony, as in auto theft court, we would hold a preliminary hearing. Upon a finding of probable cause, the case would then be sent to a felony trial court. I could tell myself that, by processing the case, I was not directly sending anyone to prison—that would be up to the felony trial assistant to do.

For a while after I was elevated to being a felony trial assistant myself, I quietly avoided trying the drug cases on our call. Since no one would suspect I was doing this, I was able to avoid the task I found to be immoral without being noticed. That could not last forever, of course. But then I was saved by electoral intervention.

In 1980, Bernard Carey was defeated by Richard M. Daley, the son of the late Richard J. Daley, the longstanding mayor and Democratic "Boss" of Chicago. Daley accused Carey of being soft on drugs, and, after his election, he created a special Drug Prosecution Unit to handle all felony drug cases in Chicago. As a result, all the cases on the dockets of the felony courtrooms, including mine, were transferred to this new unit. So I *still* did not have to prosecute any drug cases.

About the time I left the office, however, so many drug cases had been charged that the Drug Prosecution Unit became overwhelmed. Some drug cases would now return to the caseload of regular felony trial assistants. Had I stayed in the office, I would soon have had to try a drug case and either tank the case on purpose—which I would never do—or send someone to prison. But I resigned from the office before that happened. I don't claim that this was the reason I resigned when I did, but it was welcome timing.

There being two drug courts located at 26th and California, just two judges handled all the drug cases in Chicago. Inside the State's Attorney's Office, it was well known that one of them was crooked and one wasn't. The crooked judge was Wayne Olson, who sat in Branch 57. Bond-slip-hungry kink lawyers prowled the hallways outside his courtroom. Happily, my post had been to the honest judge, Arthur Zelezinski, so I did not have to contend with the corruption I'd experienced in both Branch 64 and Branch 42. Zelezinski had banned those lawyers from his courtroom.

Zelezinski's principles may have stemmed from his significant career in government. He had served as the alderman of the 12th Ward, on the city's Southwest Side, and was a close ally of Daley. Before ascending to the bench, however, he had served as the chairman of the City Council Building and Zoning Committee. There he oversaw such urban renewal projects as the University of Illinois Chicago campus and Lincoln Park. I was relieved to be assigned to his courtroom rather than to Wayne Olson's.

Olson was a hard-drinking fixture at Jean's, a bar near the courthouse where lawyers, cops, and courtroom personnel hung out and got drunk together at the end of their working day. During the day, Jean's was open to the public for lunch. After hours, however, the front door to the bar was locked, and criminal court officers would enter through the rear door off the alley. Like the "cop bars" scattered throughout the city, this was a "safe space" for carousing.

I would often eat lunch at Jean's. And while I was not a regular after-hours patron, Jean's was where we all went when we were awaiting a jury verdict.

In the days before MADD—Mothers Against Drunk Driving—court personnel who came to Jean's to drink after hours all drove home in their own cars. That included assistant state's attorneys. I was never a heavy drinker, but I would nurse a few "pops" or beers when I was there. It's remarkable what a culture shift has occurred since then. Then again, as kids we rode without any seat belts in the front seats of cars whose dashboards were made of metal, shot BB guns at each other, and played on metal jungle gyms built on asphalt. Oh, and almost every adult smoked, even pregnant women. It was, we can all agree, a different time.

"Lucius in the Box"

MY FINAL ASSIGNMENT before heading to felony trial court was to the Branch 66 homicide-sex preliminary hearing court that handled all murders and sexual assaults that happened in Chicago. Located at 26th and California, it was presided over by Judge Maurice Pompey Sr.

Pompey was a commanding presence in the courtroom, having served in World War II as one of the famed Tuskegee Airmen. But he was also notoriously corrupt. It was in Pompey's court where you could most easily fix a murder case in Cook County.

Judge Pompey's bagman—the person to whom one would pay the bribe rather than paying the person being bribed directly—was his bailiff, Lucius Robinson. Lucius would sit in the jury box to signal the judge that a payoff on that case had been made. State's attorneys would refer to a fixed case in Branch 66 as "Lucius in the box." Fortunately, none of my cases in Branch 66 were fixed. Lucius sometimes did sit in the jury box to observe court proceedings, but he never did so during one of my preliminary hearings. My friend Terry Hake, who arrived after me, was not so fortunate.

"Partner"

ONE FRIDAY, AFTER I had been in Branch 66 for a month or two, I got a phone call in my office from Irv Miller, a felony trial assistant assigned to the courtroom of Judge Eugene Pincham. Irv was one of the few Jewish ASAs at 26th Street.

"I am just calling to let you know that you have been moved up to the felony trial courts effective Monday, and are assigned to Judge Pincham's courtroom."

I was thrilled. After two years, I had finally made it to the felony trial courts and decided to celebrate by getting a beer at She-Nannigans, a bar on Division Street sometimes frequented by prosecutors. (One night I watched them film a scene for the movie *Class*, in which the absolutely drop-dead gorgeous Jacqueline Bisset was getting into a taxi just outside the bar.)

Into the bar walked a tall man I recognized as a trial assistant. I'd been around Jews all my life and figured his physiognomy made him a fellow Member of the Tribe. Which meant this could be Neil Cohen, the other Jewish trial assistant at 26th Street, or it could be Irv Miller. So I took a chance and said, "Hello, Irv." Bingo. It was him.

Irv and I were able to drink to my promotion together. We would become close friends and remain friends to this day. He attended my wedding and, after leaving the office, went on to be an effective criminal defense attorney, a legal analyst for CBS News Chicago, and a technical advisor for *The Good Wife* and *The Good Fight*.

This seems like a good place to offer a word of advice on defense attorneys.

Figure 24. Irv Miller on television *(courtesy of CBS Chicago)*

If you are ever in trouble, the kind of defense lawyer you want will depend on whether you are guilty or innocent. If you are guilty, you will want the kind of defense lawyer who can poke holes in the prosecutor's case or raise a defense that will distract the jury. Some defense lawyers, for example, specialize in "police frame" defenses whenever that argument can be made remotely plausible. That's the defense that worked for O. J. Simpson when all the physical and eyewitness evidence was against him. How do you explain away all the evidence of guilt presented by the prosecution? Why, accuse the police of planting it, of course. The stronger the evidence, the more you attribute it to the cops. But if you are guilty, you will also want a lawyer who can negotiate a good plea deal with the prosecutors.

If you are innocent, however, you will need a different kind of lawyer. Theoretically, there is a presumption of innocence in our criminal justice system. That presumption does benefit the guilty by making the prosecution prove its case. And we have already seen how the Felony Review system screens out cases that cannot be proved beyond a reasonable doubt, which also helps the innocent. But ironically, it is because of that screening that the presumption of innocence does less to protect innocent persons *who are actually charged* with a crime than it does the guilty. I realize this is counterintuitive, so let me explain the dynamic at work.

Imagine that the criminal justice system is 90 percent accurate. It is hard to imagine any government system being that accurate, but let's go with it for a moment. Given the tens of thousands of persons accused of crimes every year, a 90 percent (or even 95 percent) accuracy rate would still result in thousands of wrongfully accused defendants. But participants within the system know full well that there is a 90 percent chance of any given defendant being guilty. So this leads to a *practical* presumption of *guilt* that can only be partially mitigated by a *legal* presumption of innocence. In short, the odds are overwhelming that anyone ultimately prosecuted for a crime is actually guilty, and participants in the criminal justice system can't help but be affected by that.

Now, if you are one of the 90 percent who are guilty, you get the benefit of that legal presumption of innocence in making the prosecution prove its case. The more ideological defense attorneys motivate themselves by projecting their cynicism onto the cops and the criminal justice system so that they don't actually care if their clients are guilty or not.

But what if you are part of the 10 percent who are innocent? Well, then you're fighting against the practical presumption of guilt. For this reason, you need a lawyer who *can prove you are innocent*. I know that's not how it is supposed to work. But that's how it works.

The problem is that most criminal defense lawyers are only accustomed to knocking holes in the prosecution's case. Remember, they are used to representing the 90 percent. What you need is a defense lawyer whose skill set extends beyond poking holes in the prosecution's case. You need a defense lawyer who can prove that you are actually innocent. And that defense lawyer is very likely to have previously been a prosecutor.

Why? Due to the legal presumption of innocence, successful prosecutors must know how to build a case to prove the defendant is guilty beyond a reasonable doubt. They are constantly asking themselves the question, "Just how do I prove *X* to be true?" That is a distinct skillset, and quite different than deconstructing someone else's case.

Irv Miller became an effective defense lawyer because he was a former prosecutor who knew how to prove a case. Not only that, but because he was a former assistant state's attorney who had risen to the supervisory rank, he had credibility with ASAs. He could sometimes even get them to drop charges when he was able to establish the innocence of his client. No ASA wants to go into a trial and lose.

One of Irv's cases as a defense attorney has long stuck with me. The cops claimed to have obtained a search warrant before searching his client's home. As he always did when he was a prosecutor, especially in those pre–cell phone days, Irv subpoenaed the phone records of everyone involved with the case, including his own client. There he saw a phone call placed from his client's home phone to the home phone of one of the officers. One of the cops had called his own home from the defendant's place. But the time of that call was before the search warrant had been issued. Using this evidence, Irv was able to prove that the police first searched the house and then got the search warrant afterward. When confronted with Irv's proof that the search was illegal, the State's Attorney's Office dropped the case.

So if I were innocent and charged with a crime in Cook County, I would want my first felony trial court partner, Irv Miller, as my defense attorney. I am honored by the fact that, to this day, he still calls me "partner" whenever I see him or speak with him on the phone.

PART III: FELONY TRIAL ASSISTANT

Judge Eugene Pincham

I COULD NOT HAVE been more elated about my elevation to the trial courts and being assigned to Judge Pincham's courtroom. I had met Eugene Pincham when he was a defense attorney and I was a second-year law student clerking during the summer for the State's Attorney's Office in Judge Machala's courtroom, working with Bill Dwyer and Steve Connolly. Pincham had a case pending before Judge Machala, and, when making an appearance, he would kibbitz with me while waiting for his client's case to be called. He loved to talk.

Pincham was a tall, imposing man who enjoyed wearing a fur or leather coat, a cowboy hat, and cowboy boots. That makes an impression—although when I first met him in the courtroom, he was wearing a conservative three-piece suit. As I would learn, he had the personality to match: gregarious and charming, a true character. In a lot of ways, he reminded me of my grandfather. Like my grandfather, Pincham was both cool and a bit of an artist (con and otherwise)—you have to be if you're going to successfully defend guilty clients. He was that rare person who was larger than life.

Figure 25. Judge Eugene Pincham speaks to my Evidence class

Born on June 28, 1925, in Chicago, Illinois, Pincham grew up in impoverished conditions in Alabama, where his mother had moved following a divorce. After graduating high school in 1942, he initially attended LeMoyne College in Memphis, Tennessee, but was expelled due to poor academic performance and conduct issues. He then transferred to Tennessee State University in Nashville, where he earned a bachelor of science in political science in 1947. He married his college sweetheart Alzata C. Henry in 1948 and enrolled at Northwestern University School of Law, graduating with a JD in 1951. He would later recall that one Northwestern professor, whom he had for three classes, refused to call on him because of his skin color.

I made it a point to get to know him a bit that summer before my third year of law school, and he took an interest in me. I was even able to watch him try a jury trial. Considered one of the top criminal defense lawyers in Chicago, he was an instructor for the National Institute for Trial Advocacy (NITA) trial-advocacy program, which actual trial lawyers paid a lot of money to attend.

In the fall of my third year at Harvard, its innovative nine-hour comprehensive trial-advocacy course featured NITA instructors. One evening, Eugene Pincham gave a NITA-style lecture on making closing arguments. There he used his favorite anecdote about his mother's "sugar bowl"—an argument I had actually seen him use in court at 26th Street in service of a "police frame" defense. In his telling, he would sneak a taste of sugar by sticking his fingers in the sugar bowl when his mother was not looking. But his mother could always tell he had done it. How? Because she could see the sugar granules on the kitchen counter. Pincham would then claim that, in framing his client, the police had left granules lying around that proved they had planted the evidence. He used this childhood story to explain to a jury how circumstantial evidence proved that the cops had framed his client.

Lawyers distinguish between "direct" and "circumstantial" evidence. An example of direct evidence is when a witness testifies to seeing you commit the crime. If believed, that evidence is evidence of guilt and nothing else. Circumstantial evidence is open to more than one possible inference. A fingerprint at the scene of a crime is circumstantial evidence of your presence at some point before it was detected. But you would need other evidence to establish that it was likely only left there during the commission of the crime. Logically, it could have been left there before or after the crime was committed.

Direct evidence in the form of eyewitness testimony is known to often be unreliable. Far from being suspect, circumstantial evidence like fingerprints or DNA can actually be among the more reliable forms of evidence. Pincham's closing argument was actually a brilliant adaptation of what was really a prosecution argument about how circumstantial evidence works. Although his mother was not an eyewitness to the offense, the sugar granules lying on the counter were circumstantial evidence of what young Eugene had done (assuming, of course, that this story ever really happened).

But Eugene Pincham was a defense attorney, and he used the story as a folksy way to dramatize how the cops, to secure a conviction, might've done something illegal at the crime scene. In his telling, that circumstantial evidence showed that the cops had framed his client. After his demonstration in my class, Pincham and his wife, Alzata, took me for drinks at the bar in the newly built Charles Hotel in Harvard Square. We had a terrific time. I was genuinely flattered that he thought enough of me to take me out. Neither of us could've imagined, much less predicted, that I would one day be standing before him in a felony trial courtroom.

Shortly after speaking at Harvard, Pincham became a Cook County Circuit Court judge assigned to 26th Street. His courtroom was considered one of the toughest assignments for a state's attorney. Pincham was notoriously hard on ASAs. No prosecutor wanted to be assigned there, given how pro-defense Pincham was and how he would upbraid prosecutors for even minor mistakes.

For example, Pincham was big on courtroom decorum, which was fine by me. He had a firm rule against attorneys sitting on counsel tables while waiting for their cases to be called, which attorneys often did in other courtrooms. Also fine by me. But one day, as I was observing the call, I was standing with my arms crossed and my thigh leaning against the edge of the tabletop. Pincham turned from what he was doing at the bench and barked:

"Bailiff, would you tell that state's attorney who has been assigned to my courtroom for months, and who knows the rules, to get off that table!" Unbeknownst to me, the rule against sitting on a table also covered leaning against it.

Prosecutors tended to consider being assigned to his courtroom the equivalent of doing hard labor. But if you survived the sentence—typically three to six months—you were in line for a choice prosecutorial assignment to a pro-state judge as compensation. In fairness, Pincham could be just as hard, if not harder, on defense attorneys if he thought they weren't doing a good enough job championing their clients. Which is to say, if they weren't doing what Eugene Pincham would do if *he* were representing them.

All things being equal, the State's Attorney's Office supervisors would've loved to assign only African American prosecutors to Pincham's courtroom, given his reputation for hostility to the white state's attorneys, whom he sometimes called peacocks for how they made closing arguments. The problem was that, in those days, the State's Attorney's Office had *very* few African American prosecutors. When those few had been rotated out of his courtroom after the three-to-six-month shifts, there soon were no more to take their place. So the powers that be decided to assign the next closest thing they had: Jews and Hispanics. That's how I ended up there with the Jewish Irv Miller and the Hispanic Ron Guzmán as my partners.

What the State's Attorney's supervisors didn't realize, and what I certainly wasn't going to tell them, was that Eugene Pincham *loved* me. And I admired him. So I was thrilled to be assigned to his court. And I learned a ton from him.

Beating Jenner & Block

AS A 3RD chair, I was there to learn the ropes from the 1st chair, Irv Miller, and his 2nd chair, Ron Guzmán. (Ron recently retired from being a U.S. district court judge.) The job of the 3rd chair is to work up all the files. That meant ordering all the police reports, photos, and crime lab tests. It also sometimes meant writing legal memos.

That Monday morning, my first day on the job, everything looked familiar. Irv ran the morning call I'd seen many times thanks to my two clerkships at 26th Street: motions heard, status checks with the defense attorneys, the prosecutors, and the judge, the defendants brought in from custody, bailiffs watching, and so forth. But I was still nervous standing next to Irv as we both stood in front of the judge's bench, me for the first time as an ASA.

Figures 26–27. The ultimate goal: a felony trial courtroom at 26th and Cal

One case on the status call that morning involved a particularly heinous murder with co-defendants Sammy Lee Bynum and Joseph Cooley. Due to potential conflicts, it is standard practice for co-defendants to have separate counsel, and the public defender's office can only represent one. The other needs to be appointed by the court. (This is how former ASA Terry Ekl came to represent Juan Caballero in a multiple-defendant case.) Bynum was represented by the public defender's office. Cooley was represented by Jenner & Block, a white-shoe Chicago-based law firm with offices all over the United States and in London—the only firm I had interviewed with as a Harvard Law student.

I interviewed with Jenner because they had a unique pro bono criminal practice. The interviewer was Tom Sullivan, who went on to be the U.S. Attorney for the Northern District of Illinois. Sullivan could not conceal his lack of interest in hiring me. When I left the room, I kicked myself for breaking my vow of avoiding law firms. So I had a bit of a chip on my shoulder when it came to Jenner & Block.

Most of Jenner's criminal work was white-collar stuff, to go along with their transactional business and litigation. But they had an aggressive pro bono commitment that cleverly provided their best partners and associates with courtroom experience defending criminal defendants of all kinds. And in those pro bono cases, they had the vast resources of the firm behind them. Of course, it was no shame for Jenner to lose these cases in which evidence of guilt was usually overwhelming. What counted was the experience the case provided its lawyers, and the publicity for the firm.

In this case, the two black defendants were charged with abducting a black man as he came out of a bodega where he had bought some milk for his family, then bringing him back to his apartment, hog-tying the man and his wife, and shooting both in the head in front of their two very young children. The egregiousness of the crime affected everyone involved with it, including Eugene Pincham. The case was considered a "death case"—meaning the State's Attorney's Office would seek the death penalty.

But this wasn't a clean case. The problems with it could be traced to what we called *stranger homicide,* meaning that there was no connection between the perpetrators and the victims. Most murder victims and their murderers are known to each other. Here, the defendants were complete strangers. The cops had had nothing to go on except what little they could get out of the traumatized children. The cops had to resort to asking everyone they came in contact with if they knew anything.

The investigating detectives even went into the police station lockups, gathered the prisoners, and asked if anyone knew anything or had overheard anything from someone who might've talked about doing the crime or even bragged about it. Finally, one guy in a lockup, Joseph Cooley, raised his hand and said he'd heard so-and-so did it. The detective asked where he could find so-and-so, and Cooley said he'd be able to take the cops to him. Based on that claim, the detective signed him out of lockup to have him help find the perpetrators in exchange for consideration on whatever offense had put him behind bars.

Everywhere Cooley took the cops, however, the guy he said did it wasn't to be found. The cops kept up with what soon became apparent was Kabuki because the guy seemed to know an awful lot about the case that he couldn't have known unless he really had heard something or—wait a second—what if *he* did it?

As soon as this possibility dawned on them, the investigators read Cooley his *Miranda* rights, at which point he confessed and named Bynum as his partner. Confronted with what Cooley had told them, Bynum subsequently also confessed. The two confessions contained every detail that confirmed conclusively for the detectives that these weren't false confessions from men looking for some consideration. So case closed, right? Not so fast.

On my first day as a felony trial assistant, the Jenner & Block attorneys showed up with a motion to suppress the confessions on the grounds that they were initiated without *Miranda* warnings. *Miranda* was commonly understood to require the right-to-remain-silent warnings given whenever there was a "custodial interrogation." In this case, there was no question that Cooley had been in custody (on another charge) when he was first questioned. Once the suspect was in custody, *Miranda* was normally interpreted to automatically apply due to the coercive nature of the interaction. But it wasn't just Cooley's confession that was at issue. If Bynum confessed as a result of hearing that Cooley had, his confession would be considered "fruit of the poisonous tree," even though he had been given his *Miranda* rights before confessing.

And the stakes could not have been higher. No physical evidence or eyewitness testimony tied either Bynum or Cooley to the murder. The case rested entirely on the confessions.

When the Jenner attorney handed Irv our copy of their motion, Irv immediately turned and handed it to me, saying, "Here's your first assignment. You have to respond to this."

In pre-internet days, researching something like this required going physically into a law library and picking through big, thick books. No electronic searching. LexisNexis had just arrived but was still primitive, and I had not gotten skilled in using it.

My research in the State's Attorney's library went on for days in between my other tasks, sometimes into the evening. I was motivated by the fact that what the police had done here seemed completely reasonable to me. And the law doesn't usually punish reasonable actions. But intuitions would not be enough. I needed a theory of *why* it seemed reasonable.

True, Bynum was definitely in custody. And it did not matter what he was in custody for. But the operative term was "custodial *interrogation*." His exchanges with the detectives didn't seem like interrogations to me. They seemed like, well, *conversations*. But I hadn't heard of any such distinction governing *Miranda* warnings.

It was just a theory, and a state-minded judge might have bought it. But a mere theory would not be enough to satisfy a pro-defense judge like Pincham. Nor would pointing out that Cooley had already been Mirandized when he was taken into custody for the other crime for which he was jailed when the police first contacted him. Again, that might have been enough for a state-minded judge, but not for Eugene Pincham. We needed something more on point, or these two murderers would walk. Their confessions were essentially all the evidence we had, and Pincham was fearless enough to grant a motion to suppress that had merit, as this one appeared to have, even in so egregious a case. Recall that Pincham was the judge who'd acquitted Luis Ruiz of murder after a bench trial. Most circuit court judges would have admitted the statements, held a trial, and let the appellate court sort out their admissibility. Pincham was not like most judges.

But then I came upon *U.S. v. Wiggins*, which was based on facts that were stunningly similar to our case. Like Cooley, Wiggins kept digging himself deeper by sending the investigating officers down the wrong track until it was clear that he was the perpetrator. The cops had had no reason to suspect Wiggins of being the offender until Wiggins's own words and actions led them to that conclusion. He and the cops were engaged in a conversation, not an interrogation. The U.S. Court of Appeals for the D.C Circuit concluded that, while Wiggins was in custody, he "was neither a suspect nor a prospective subject. ... There was nothing to suggest that the *Miranda* warnings were required because nothing suggested that Wiggins himself was the guilty man." So being in custody did not automatically make the conversation with the cops into a custodial interrogation.

The only arguable difference between the facts of my case and that of *Wiggins* was who spoke first. In my case, the cops spoke first, asking if anyone knew anything about the murder. By contrast, Wiggins had asked to speak to the cops. But that didn't matter; in my memo in opposition to the motion to suppress, I still argued that "since Cooley was not a suspect, the interview with him, though he was in custody, was not an interrogation." "For that reason," I concluded, *Miranda* warnings, which are "required before any custodial interrogation were not required here."

Irv and Ron were thrilled. The guys from Jenner & Block less so. They simply did not expect an Assistant Cook County State's Attorney to file the kind of response I filed.

Linda Listrom, an HLS classmate of mine, now worked at Jenner and happened to be dating one of the guys on the trial team. "Who *is* this guy?" he asked her.

"I'll Never Fry Those Boys"

JUDGE PINCHAM WAS impressed as well. Pro-defendant as he was, he was also against the stone-cold murder of two parents in front of their kids. He needed the goods, however, and I had provided them. That solidified his respect for me.

In a three-person courtroom, two prosecutors try each jury case. It is up to the 1st chair to decide which pair. When one saves a case the way I did, it was expected that I would 2nd-chair this trial—which is what Irv told me would happen if we went to trial.

As a kid, I had been in favor of the death penalty. It seemed infinitely clear to me that some crimes were so heinous that, by committing them, the criminals had forfeited their right to life. But then, as I became a libertarian (both capital and small *L*), I changed my mind. I concluded that state-sponsored executions, being premeditated, were a form of murder. Among my earliest scholarship was an article titled "Restitution: A New Paradigm of Criminal Justice," which was published in the philosophy journal *Ethics* in 1977. In it, I advocated replacing retribution or punishment—the deliberate infliction of harm to criminals—with compelling criminals to make reparations or restitution to their victims and their survivors, in this case, the children of the murdered couple here.

How then could I justify being a criminal prosecutor in a system in which the ultimate end being sought was the punishment of the guilty? Simple. Justice required that the guilty had to pay *somehow*, that *something* had to happen to them, that they not escape any consequences for violating the rights of others. If restitution is off the table, then between their going to prison and going scot-free, I favored prison.

Eventually, I modified my position. In my 1998 book, *The Structure of Liberty*, I concluded that the principle of restitution to victims of crime needed to be supplemented by the concept of societal self-defense. People who, by their behavior, had proven themselves to be a "standing threat" to the rights of others could justly be made incapable of committing more crimes. Properly conceived, "incapacitation"—as it was called by philosophers of punishment—was not inflicted as a punishment, but as self-defense. Imprisonment could be inflicted as punishment; but it also served to incapacitate the offender by removing him from the community. But we, the innocent, were not obligated to incapacitate stone-cold murderers like Henry Brisbon, or Bynum and Cooley, by housing them indefinitely at taxpayer expense. They could be more permanently removed from society, as they had removed their victims. By death.

In 1979, however, I had not yet reached this conclusion. As a prosecutor, I was conflicted. I for sure wanted to try this big case. But I had qualms about asking a jury to do something I did not think was moral. If anyone in my office learned of my reservation, I would be out as a felony trial assistant. But if I kept my reservations to myself, I could likely avoid being put into a position of conflict by declining to 2nd-chair the case. After all, the competition to handle capital cases was intense. That, however, would have been awkward.

As a law clerk, I had indiscreetly admitted my view on the death penalty to someone—quite possibly Lee Shalgos, an ASA who in 1974 had prosecuted the man who held up my grandfather and my brother at gunpoint in my grandfather's tile store in Harvey, Illinois. Lee had recommended me for my first summer clerkship, but he constantly hung around the State's Attorney's offices at 26th Street visiting his buddies. His buddies included Mike Ficaro, who was then the supervisor of our wing at 26th Street. By the time I reached the felony trial courts, Ficaro was the chief of the criminal trial courts and was responsible for all the assignments. Thanks to him, I moved up rapidly through the ranks.

Like virtually all prosecutors, Ficaro had no qualms about the death penalty. To the contrary, he was an enthusiastic supporter. Recall that Ficaro had prosecuted Henry Brisbon, the cold-blooded I-57 murderer. *Time* quoted Ficaro as saying: "On the day he dies in the chair at Stateville, I plan to be there to see that it's done. Nobody I've heard of deserves the death penalty more than Henry Brisbon."

Only after I left the prosecutor's office did I learn that Ficaro had been informed of my stance on the death penalty. Fortunately for me, he did not hold it against me. As I later learned, this was his response to being told: "Don't worry. He's young. He'll grow out of it." Years later, at a state's attorneys' reunion, I had the chance to thank him for this.

Grow out of it I did, but ironically not until I entered legal academia, where opposition to the death penalty was *de rigueur*. I characterize myself as a contrarian, and this is a good example of my contrarianism. When I was a college student among "liberals," I was pro-death penalty. By the time I was a prosecutor among death-penalty supporters, I was against it. Then, after I entered academia, where the death penalty was anathematic, I supported it again.

One of the greatest things about the whole six months I spent in Judge Pincham's court was that he allowed me to hang with him in his chambers in between cases and in the afternoons after the court call ended. I'd listen to him pontificate the way he used to when I was a law student, dissecting many of the cases on the call from the point of view of a defense attorney. I just soaked it up, knowing that one of a prosecutor's most valuable skills is the ability to evaluate what a case looks like from the defense's point of view. The more we chatted over the months, the more he confided.

Now it was my turn to confide in him.

"Judge," I said, "I've got a problem here. I don't believe in the death penalty, and this is a death penalty case. So I don't know what to do."

Without hesitating, he replied, "You've got to try this case." Period.

"Why?" I asked him.

"Because you earned it. It's a great case to try. You need to try this case."

"Well, I just don't know if I can do that because I don't know if I can get up in front of a jury and ask them to do something that I myself have a moral objection to."

And now it was the judge's turn to confide in me something that was, in the Cook County justice system, riskier for him to admit than what I'd confided to him was for me.

"Don't worry," he said, "I'll never fry those boys."

I was as stunned as I was relieved. I was also honored by his trust in me. What he'd just told me, if it had gotten out, might very well have gotten him transferred out of the felony trial courts. And full circuit court judges in Illinois have to stand for reelection. That admission could cost him his job.

Moreover, the death penalty was and is one of the strongest bargaining chips a prosecutor has in his bag. So, too, with a judge who wants to get a plea bargain in a case in his courtroom. Taking it off the table in exchange for a guilty plea is done all the time. Pincham wanted the defendants to plead guilty. So he did not want it known that he would never sentence them to death.

Which was why, after we won the motion that kept the confessions in, the Jenner & Block attorneys began negotiating to plea these guys down to hefty prison sentences instead of the electric chair. Bynum and Cooley got eighty years apiece. And I never had to reconcile my moral conundrum.

* * *

On December 2, 1979, right after I had reached the felony trial courts and was assigned to Judge Pincham's courtroom, Beth and I were married at the Drake Hotel on Lake Shore Drive. We had been dating since the summer between my second and third years of law school, after having been fixed up on a blind date by our fathers. My high school best friend, Jay Blackburn, was my best man. My groomsmen were my brother Howard, my law school roommate Larry Bailin, my law school libertarian compatriot John Hagel, and my good friend and fellow Assistant State's Attorney Terry Hake. Judge John Crowley and his wife, Bette, were also there.

Figure 28. My bride Beth, and my groomsmen *(From left to right, Mark Black, Larry Bailin, Howard Barnett, Terry Hake, Jay Blackburn and John Hagel III)*

I remember getting my hair cut for the wedding by a stylist on Oak Street I had patronized since college. Also at the salon that day was Dean Wolfson. Wolfson was a silver-haired attorney who always wore a well-tailored three-piece suit. He was also known to be a very high-end fixer, unlike the rats that prowled the hallways for bond slips. He would never try a case. If he couldn't fix it, he would pass it along to another attorney. His nickname was "Dean the Dream." As I recall, Dean was at the salon to be groomed for his daughter's wedding.

Sometime after this, I was approached by someone—I cannot recall who—who told me he had a message for me from Wolfson. I should stop "bad-mouthing him" as a corrupt lawyer. This struck me as bizarre. For one thing, though I certainly believed him to be corrupt, I did not recall ever bad-mouthing him to others. For another, *everyone* knew he was a fixer, so why single me out for such a warning?

I never found out.

The Mouse in the Courtroom

MY FIRST FELONY jury trial concerned a "caught-inside" burglary of an apartment by one Raymond Harding. I tried the case as 2nd chair to Ron Guzmán. It was noteworthy only for the fact that the jury was hung 11–1, making it my only felony jury trial that did not result in a guilty verdict. Before the trial, Harding had been offered a reduced sentence in return for him waiving his right to a trial and pleading guilty. Instead, he decided to roll the dice on a jury trial. Coming so close to being convicted changed his mind. After the mistrial he pled guilty in return for a reduced sentence, so there was no second trial.

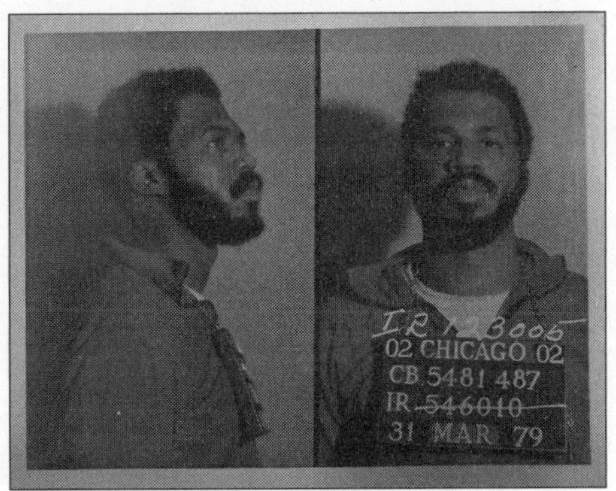

Figure 29. Raymond Harding
(courtesy of Chicago Police Department)

But this was not my most memorable courtroom experience in Judge Pincham's court. My most memorable experience wasn't even a case I tried. It was a case tried by Irv and Ron that I observed. What follows are the facts as reported by the Illinois Court of Appeals:

> On May 11, 1977, at approximately 3:15 p.m., the defendant [Julius Anderson] surprised the victim when she was alone in her apartment on the north side of Chicago. At gunpoint [Anderson] robbed the victim, then bound her hands behind her back with nylon stockings. After [he] discovered that the victim's roommate had a few hundred dollars in a bank account, defendant told her that they would wait until the roommate came home from work, then all three of them would drive to the bank where the roommate would withdraw her funds.
>
> While they were waiting, [Anderson], placing the loaded revolver to the victim's temple and threatening

> to "blow her brains out," forced the victim to submit to acts of anal and sexual intercourse. [He] put on one of the victim's sweaters, then went into her roommate's closet and removed a pair of blue jeans.
>
> Concerned that the victim's roommate might not be so easily subdued, [Anderson] decided to leave before she returned from work. He placed the victim in the hall closet, blocking it with a desk, rummaged around in the apartment for a few minutes, then left. The victim escaped and ran to another apartment for help. Later that day a physician at St. Francis Hospital in Evanston found evidence of spermatozoa in her vaginal area.
>
> The following afternoon, [Anderson] was arrested by the Evanston police who had spotted a handgun in his waistband and had observed him wearing the sweater and jeans he had removed from the apartment. A search of [Anderson] yielded other property taken in the robbery. [He] was thereafter identified in a lineup and his fingerprints were matched to those developed at the scene.

When a case is this open and shut, the insanity defense becomes one of the only potentially viable options. There was no question about whether Julius Anderson was the perpetrator of this sexual assault. The only question was his state of mind.

The case was tried by Irv Miller and Ron Guzmán, and it fell to Ron to cross-examine the psychiatrist defense expert named Jerome Katz. Ron did so masterful a job that I asked the court reporter to prepare a transcript of Katz's testimony, which a few years later I would have my students read when I taught Evidence at the Chicago-Kent College of Law—my first teaching gig. Even today, rereading the examination leaves me impressed.

Ron began by challenging the relationship between the psychosis diagnosed by the doctor and the legal definition of insanity. The doctor came off as deeply confused. Ron then challenged the efficacy of diagnosing such mental states by invoking a study in which twelve persons were instructed to lie to psychiatrists about their mental states, which resulted in all twelve being confined to mental institutions. While there, they behaved perfectly normally, but staff interpreted their normal behavior as consistent with their diagnosed conditions. Eventually, they had to be released by intervention by those who ran the study. (For technical reasons, the court of appeals would later hold this line of questioning to be in error, though harmless.)

In one particularly memorable exchange, Ron probed the doctor about whether he thought the defendant might have been trying to deceive him. The doctor conceded that the defendant seemed to be exaggerating some of his symptoms.

"The question is, Doctor, do you think that he exaggerated any of his symptoms in order to try to make you believe and testify that he was legally insane at the time that he committed the offense?"

The doctor answered, "I don't know if that was in his mind."

"Doctor," replied Ron, "the entire purpose of the examination was to determine his state of mind, wasn't it?"

I nearly laughed out loud at the doctor's answer. *"I don't know if that was in his mind"?* Here, the witness was testifying to Anderson's state of mind a year before, but could not say what his state of mind was when the defendant was sitting right in front of him. (Believe me, this brief summary does not do justice to the devastating nature of this cross-examination.)

Pincham was clearly offended by the shoddiness of the testimony and impressed by the skillfulness of Ron's cross-examination. Afterward, in chambers, he told Ron, "You ripped that man a new asshole." For better or worse, Pincham conveyed his attitude to the jury, as frequently happens. Unlike what you see on TV courtroom dramas, lawyers know that judges have a way of punishing them in front of a jury when they annoy or displease the judge.

At one point during the cross-examination, the public defender, Ronald Katz (no relation to the witness, Dr. Jerome Katz), objected to the tone of Ron's questioning, an objection calculated to disparage opposing counsel's technique and to disrupt his momentum. "I would ask the Court to instruct Counsel to keep a civil tone in this courtroom," he said.

Pincham was having none of this. The exchange that follows tells you more about what a character Pincham was than anything else I can relate:

"You're instructed to keep a civil tone," Pincham began, speaking to Ron. "I have not heard you use anything but a civil tone, but Mr. Katz wants me to instruct you to do that so I will grant the motion. I do not imply that your tone has been anything other than civil. Mr. Katz may but I don't. Proceed, please."

Ron then responded, "Thank you, Judge. I promise the Court I will do so."

Which led Pincham to continue, "You can raise your voice up, and down if you want, that's your prerogative of cross-examination. Do it the way you want to do it. Just don't shout so loud you hurt our eardrums. All right."

Ron then resumed his cross, "Doctor, when you—" But Pincham was now on a roll:

"That's what makes cross-examination fun, isn't it? Do it the way you want to do it."

"I hope so. I hope so," replied Ron a bit sheepishly.

"Overruled, Mr. Katz," Pincham responded, telling Ron to "go ahead." With that, cross-examination finally resumed.

Pincham's ultimate disrespect of the expert witness was manifested by an occurrence that was tailor-made for the screen, written by the endlessly inventive former lawyer David E. Kelley. Indeed, I would not believe a lawyer if he told me this story (which is another reason I requested a transcript).

To fully appreciate what happened, you need to understand the layout of the courtroom. The judge sat on the bench. Somewhat below him to his left (to the right as you were facing the bench) was the witness stand, which is also called a "witness box." In front of the witness was a low wall or barrier that made it a "box." Perpendicular to the witness box, the jury sat against the wall to the left as you were facing the bench. The jury box was open on the end facing the witness so the jurors could turn their chairs and face the witness to their right.

As Doctor Katz was being systematically demolished, a mouse ran

Figure 30. View of jury box from witness stand

into the courtroom and perched on the floor in front of the witness box. The jurors could see the mouse and reacted viscerally, physically shrinking away from it. But Dr. Katz could not see the mouse because the front of the witness box blocked his view. All he could see was the jurors shrinking away from him as though they were repelled by his testimony.

When Pincham saw the jurors' reactions, he stood up and saw the mouse. Here is how the transcript reads:

> THE COURT: "Are you aware of what's going on?"
> MR. GUZMAN: "I am afraid I do."
> THE COURT: "I wasn't." (Referring to mouse in courtroom.)

In this way, Pincham acknowledged the situation while being careful not to clue the witness into what was happening. For all Dr. Katz knew, the jurors were shrinking away from him in horror due to the pounding he was taking during cross-examination.

Julius Anderson was convicted of rape. For this and some other pending cases, he was sentenced by Judge Pincham to serve seven years for burglary, thirty years for armed robbery, thirty-five years for rape, and forty years for deviate sexual assault. In 2009, at the age of fifty-nine, he was paroled to a halfway house. According to ABC News, "On Aug. 7, 2009, six weeks after arriving, Anderson asked state parole officials for permission to leave and was denied, records show. He removed an electronic monitoring bracelet and left without permission, records show."

Within three months, he had committed at least three other sexual assaults. ABC News reported:

> In the first, early the morning of Aug. 15, 2009, a 25-year-old woman was held at knife point and forced into a gangway near West Cornelia and North Marshfield, where she was sexually assaulted, prosecutors said. The second attack occurred three days later when Anderson choked a 28-year-old woman to force his way into her apartment, where he tied her with nylon cord, removed her clothing and fondled her, prosecutors allege. He then told her she was going to die, but fled the apartment. In the third attack on Sept. 1, a 28-year-old woman was grabbed as she entered her apartment, forced into a bedroom and bound with electrical tape, prosecutors allege. Anderson removed her clothing with a knife, cut her breast, sexually assaulted her, then stole several items and fled.

For these three assaults, he was sentenced to seventy-five years' imprisonment. The victims filed a civil suit for negligence against the halfway house. They also sued the two psychologists who recommended that Anderson be released to the halfway house. Psychology, it seemed, was no match for whatever was in Julius Anderson's mind.

* * *

If there was a downside to being a prosecutor in Eugene Pincham's courtroom, it was the rarity of jury trials. For cases that were actually close enough to warrant a trial, defense attorneys usually figured they were better off taking a bench trial with Pincham. They knew the judge believed in the presumption of innocence, was skeptical of cops and prosecutors, and had the guts to acquit defendants on the basis of reasonable doubt. Most judges who have to run for reelection would, of course, rather the jury did the politically risky work.

To help me gain jury trial experience during this time, Patrick O'Brien, the 1st chair ASA in Judge Thomas Maloney's courtroom, asked me to 2nd-chair two jury trials there. This was the same Judge Maloney who'd substituted for Judge Crowley in Branch 43. Though I worried I had lost all credibility with him, in fact, he considered me to have integrity as a prosecutor.

In turn, I respected him as a no-nonsense trial judge. He controlled his courtroom and made sound evidentiary rulings. A former criminal defense lawyer, Maloney was neither pro-prosecution nor pro-defense. I remember him standing behind his black leather chair on the bench as he listened to evidence, which was a real power move. On the wall behind him hung a painting of Chief Justice John Marshall. True to his word, he always treated me with respect that dated back to our shared experience in Branch 43.

Wesley Spann, the first defendant I tried in front of him, was charged with auto theft of a van. The most memorable part of the case was the fact that Spann was a baseball groupie who would hang out at the hotels where visiting pro baseball teams were staying when in town to play the Cubs or White Sox. We joked that "baseball had been very, very bad" for Wesley (an adaptation of a *Saturday Night Live* skit featuring Garrett Morris as a baseball player). The jury found Spann guilty of felony possession.

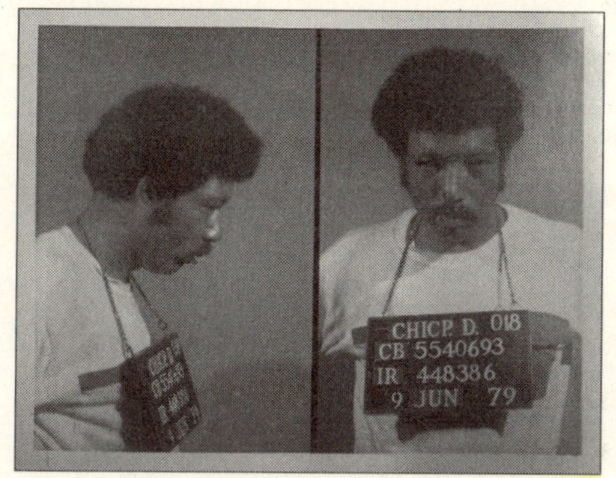

Figure 31. Wesley Spann
(courtesy of Chicago Police Department)

The other case involved Anthony Flowers and Katherine Jackson. Flowers and Jackson were charged with murdering Lonnie Butts, a drug dealer they'd bought from. They killed him to steal his drugs and cash—not the last such case I would try. Flowers hit Butts in the head with a metal bar, and Jackson then stabbed him to death with a knife. Both were found guilty of murder. The female murderer was more bloodthirsty than her male partner, which is not as uncommon as you might imagine. While most violent criminals are males, those females who cross the line can be particularly ruthless.

Over a six-month span in which I was assigned to Judge Pincham's courtroom, I managed to get three jury trials under my belt, which ain't bad. I was then in line to be rewarded for my "hard time" there.

Figure 32. Anthony Flowers
(courtesy of Chicago Police Department)

Cook County Corruption Hits Too Close to Home

WHILE I WAS still assigned to Judge Pincham's courtroom, my buddy Terry Hake visited me in my office to tell me that he was being transferred to narcotics court. What? Terry had already made it to the felony trial courts, being assigned to the newly opened felony courtrooms at 13th and Michigan. Nobody who's doing the job well—and I assumed he was—gets transferred back down to drug court. Even if they'd screwed up badly, they'd get fired, not transferred back to a minor-league assignment.

I was dumbfounded and asked him why. With a kind of hangdog look, he said, "Well, Ficaro knew that I haven't been very happy in the job." So rather than allowing him to quit, Ficaro—for whom Terry had worked the I-57 murder case—had told him he was going to take the pressure off of him by sending him back down "where it's going to be easier for you."

Maybe the pressure had gotten to him in a way I couldn't read. This struck me as very strange, but heck, there was a lot of pressure on ASAs, and Terry was a nice, decent guy. Maybe he was just not tough enough for the job. It happens.

Drug court was located at 26th Street, where I was now assigned. Soon I noticed Terry hanging out with the drug court lawyers I knew to be crooked from my time in Branch 25. These were the guys who trolled the hallways for clients to ensnare in their bond money schemes, collecting the client's bond money after a payoff to Judge Wayne Olson and subsequent acquittal. As I left the building at lunchtime, I would often see Terry and one or more of them going to lunch together at Jean's.

One of those lawyers was Jim Costello, a tall, gangly white man with an Afro-like hairdo. I knew Costello was one of the hallway fixers in Judge Olson's courtroom. While driving somewhere, I asked Terry why he was hanging out with that slimeball.

"He's not such a bad guy," Terry said.

Really? I thought. Terry's blithe response disturbed me. After that conversation, I could not get "He's not such a bad guy" out of my head.

As the months rolled by, Terry became a regular partner of Costello and the other fixers at Jean's. I knew that many of these fixers were former ASAs from the bad old days. Costello was a former ASA. That meant that some percentage of the prosecutors with whom I worked would give in to the allure of easy cash payoffs and become kinks as Matt had. Knowing this, I assumed that eventually someone with whom I served would end up as a corrupt fixer lawyer. But Terry was the last guy in the world I would've thought of as corruptible, let alone corrupted.

But now that it had happened, I thought, *Well, Terry was a nice guy. Maybe too nice.* He never struck me as a hard-charging, tough prosecutor. "Peacocks" is what Pincham called those kinds of prosecutors, the ones who enjoyed sticking their fingers in the faces of defendants during closing arguments. I did not aspire to that. But I did aspire to being appropriately tough. I now saw Terry's soft-spoken niceness as weakness—too weak to resist the corruption that pervaded the system.

Once I saw Terry associating with the lawyers I knew were already kinks, I knew I had to stop associating with Terry. I stopped calling him, and he never called me. It was truly sad. Sometime after, Terry left the State's Attorney's Office for private practice, joining Costello and the other fixers in the hallways of Branch 57 and God knew where else. Since we were no longer hanging out, I was not paying close attention to his comings and goings. He was dead to me.

Cook County corruption had struck way too close to home. One of my groomsmen at my wedding, for Chrissake. How could I have been so bad a judge of character?

The Worst Performance of My Career

MY REWARD FOR doing well in Eugene Pincham's court was an assignment as 3rd chair in Judge Frank Barbaro's court. Barbaro was known to be a pro-state judge, meaning a prosecutors' judge, but not a pushover. Barbaro, a 1948 graduate of DePaul University College of Law, grew up in Chicago's Bridgeport neighborhood, where Richard "Boss" Daley lived and raised his family. Barbaro left Bridgeport for Orland Park, where my parents had moved from Calumet City. He served as both a Cook County public defender and an assistant state's attorney. For eight years, he presided over a courtroom at 26th Street as a circuit court judge, where he earned the nickname "Bar-B-Q Barbaro" for his tough sentencing.

Yet after Barbaro's death in 1997, Stuart Nudelman, the public defender assigned to his courtroom when I was there, described him as "very, very tough, but he was fair and he believed in the law." Nudelman became a circuit court judge and succeeded Barbaro as chief judge of the Maybrook branch of the circuit court, the position Barbaro held after sitting at 26th Street. Nudelman added that Barbaro "taught me about the law and, more important, about being honest and *doing the right thing*."

"Doing the right thing" was the watchword of stand-up judges, prosecutors, and public defenders. It did not, as some would have it, mean stepping outside the law to get a "just" result. It meant doing justice according to the law when you might pay a personal or professional price for doing that. ASAs were *expected* by the supervisors to "do the right thing" on their own initiative. To suffer any bad consequences should matters go south was understood to be just part of the job.

For example, when one's supervisors would not approve dropping or reducing the charges for fear of political blowback should that defendant go on to commit a crime, "doing the right thing" could mean arranging with the defense and the judge for a "stipulated" bench trial. In a stipulated bench trial, the evidence is read into the record by the ASA and "stipulated" by the defense. The judge would then find a defendant not guilty—or guilty of a lesser offence. Of course, this meant that the trial judge, rather than the State's Attorney's Office, would take the heat, which judges resented.

In Judge Barbaro's courtroom, the 1st chair was Kenny Malatesta—Italian, like Barbaro—and Bill H., an Arab American. Whether he was Muslim or Christian, I don't know, but Bill was hostile to me from day one.

Kenny was a tough-talking, streetwise kind of guy and highly effective as a prosecutor. He had been born and raised on Chicago's Near West Side, and he served in the United States Army before getting his JD, like Barbaro, from DePaul. He and Bill had formed a close friendship. In truth, I don't think either of them liked me very much, but Kenny generally rose above whatever antipathy he had. Bill, not so much.

Sadly, the dynamics of the relationship infected and affected my performance. In fact, my single worst performance as a prosecutor was in this court, during a jury trial—a performance that also represents my single worst performance as a professional in any professional endeavor I put effort and intention into trying to do well.

In April of 1980, Kenny and I tried a rape case. The defendant, John Freeman, had kidnapped a young respiratory therapist named Rasheead, who was standing at a bus stop, by forcing her at gunpoint into the car. He drove to a secluded spot, ordered her out of the car, and raped her. After this, he ordered her into the trunk of the car wearing only her socks and shoes. He drove around the city, stopping four times to repeat the acts in various locations. The whole attack took place over three hours, during which time he raped her vaginally, orally, and anally. His trunk lid was secured by wires, and, at some point, she was able to get the lid open enough to stick her hand out and wave for help, but to no avail. Eventually, he released her, partially clad and blindfolded, and told her to run down the alley or he would "blow her head off."

Rasheead tried to cover herself with her torn blouse and, as luck would have it, was soon able to flag down a passing patrol car. She described the defendant, his clothes, and the car's broken trunk lid to the police. With Rasheead in the back seat, the officers started driving around to locate the car with its tied-down trunk, which the arresting officer testified he did approximately five minutes after finding the victim. Freeman was wearing the pinstriped pants that Rasheead had described to them. She identified Freeman on the spot as her assailant and pleaded with the officer, "Please don't put that man in the car with me."

The defense attorney put his client on the stand, a rare occurrence. But with a case as strong as ours, the defendant had little to lose. During direct examination, Freeman claimed that he was drinking at his friend Larry's house, and another man named Louis Keys had taken his car for a drive. Freeman said he was stopped by the cops only after Louis returned it to him and he was checking the car to see if any damage had been done.

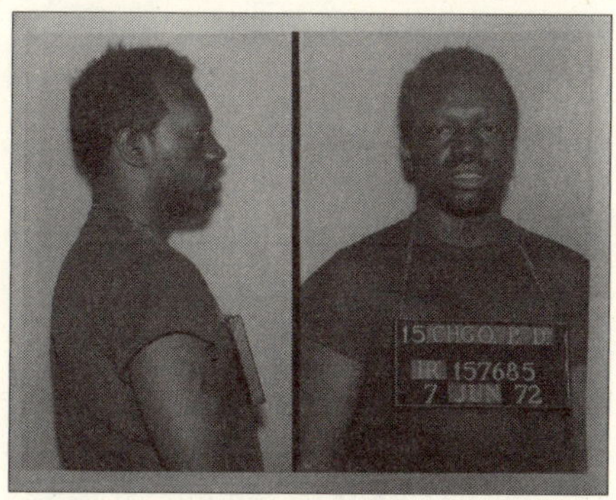

Figure 33. John Freeman
(courtesy of Chicago Police Department)

This was what we called the "S.O.D.D.I." defense: Some Other Dude Did It.

Kenny tasked me with cross-examining Freeman, which was an honor usually reserved for the 1st chair. I'd never cross-examined a defendant in front of a jury.

Disaster ensued.

Out of the corner of my eye, I could see Kenny putting his face in his hands, which of course he shouldn't have done, as it sends a signal to the jury, but I suppose I couldn't blame him; it was a reflex, like your lower leg kicking when the doctor hammers your knee.

When I stood to cross the defendant, I just lit into him. On a one-to-ten scale, I started at eleven. This was *not* the way to cross-examine anyone, including the most hardened criminals. In front of a jury, you want to start slowly and build toward a destination, typically the point where the witness says something he claims to have witnessed or you know to be a lie. And until a witness says something that *justifies* an emotional response, you don't escalate; you don't get ahead of him. But when you start at eleven, there is nowhere to go. The whole time it was happening, I knew how badly it was going, but I couldn't right the ship.

Interestingly, I had conducted cross-examinations and direct examinations of witnesses many times and done it well. That this was the defendant seemed to be what threw me off, combined with the insecurity that resulted in the teasing from Kenny and Bill. I was trying to prove myself to Kenny. Looking back today, I think Kenny's hazing of me was pretty normal stuff for the State's Attorney's Office (though nothing like that had happened with Irv and Ron, so it was unexpected). I think it was Bill's pretty naked antagonism that fueled my insecurity and response.

At any rate, I learned that day how *not* to cross-examine a defendant by doing it all wrong.

In real time.

The only thing that mitigated my performance was the verdict.

"Guilty," said the foreman.

Judge Barbaro sentenced John Freeman to fifty years in the penitentiary for rape.

This suggests something about how the attorney's trial performance is not as important to the outcome of a case as are the facts and evidence. But my Harvard instructor Nick Littlefield would admonish us that the positive outcome does not mitigate the failure to do the job right.

Because defendants rarely took the stand, prosecutors rarely had the opportunity to cross-examine them. Indeed, defendants rarely put on many witnesses in their defense. Conversely, because they rarely offer their own witnesses, criminal defense attorneys are not always as skillful as prosecutors in conducting direct examinations, in which leading questions are a big no-no.

It was nine months until I had another opportunity to cross-examine a defendant and test whether I was right about what I thought my mistake had been. It was during that period that I diagnosed the problem as rather simple: a failure to build emotionally and to await a response from the witness that merited an emotional escalation. The next opportunity, I did it right and all went well.

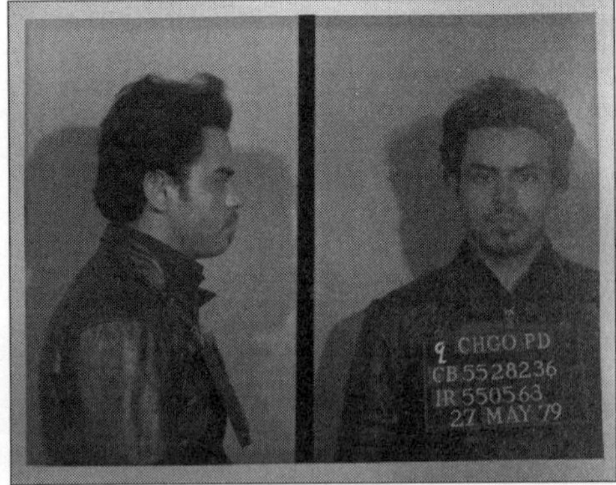

Figure 34. Antonio Gonzalez
(courtesy of Chicago Police Department)

Lesson learned. But an embarrassing memory.

Kenny and I did have another jury trial together. Antonio Gonzalez shot and killed Roy Arias when Arias attempted to stop Gonzalez from stealing his father's car. The victim's family had attended the whole trial. After closing arguments, I took them to Jean's to await the verdict, which came well into the evening. Guilty of murder. I remember how grateful they were for my performance in the courtroom on their behalf.

Voter Fraud

AS MENTIONED EARLIER, I had flirted with the idea of being a philosophy professor instead of a lawyer. A career writing about justice and liberty struck me as appealing. But for a number of reasons, I decided to stay the course and become a criminal lawyer. In my application to Harvard Law, however, I stated my ambition to be a law professor and teach jurisprudence or the philosophy of law. So a career as a law professor was always in the back of my mind.

Still, when I became a prosecutor, I resolved to put aside all such thoughts and to do the job 100 percent. I told myself that in the future, when I met a prosecutor, I would be able to shake his or her hand and say, "I was a prosecutor, too," and really mean it; that I was no dilettante, but was a criminal trial lawyer. Whenever I speak to a judicial conference or bar association, I always start by letting them know that I was not just a pointy-headed intellectual; I used to be a real lawyer.

In the summer after my third year in the State's Attorney's Office, something happened to deflect my attention. After serving on the board of directors of the Center for Libertarian Studies during my first year of law school, I had been deeply involved with the Institute for Humane Studies (IHS). IHS had given me a "Law and Liberty Fellowship" to write about restitution to victims of crime in the summer between my first and second years of law school. That paper was published in *Ethics*. After I took the bar exam, I awaited the results in Menlo Park, California (where the IHS was then located), having been given another fellowship. During that time, I wrote a follow-up paper on restitution that was published in the *American Journal of Jurisprudence*.

In those days, IHS was committed to nurturing future libertarian intellectuals starting when they were undergrads. So when my good friend Walter Grinder asked me to lecture on law at one of the first IHS "Liberty and Society" summer seminars for undergraduates, I could not decline. I took one week of vacation time over the summer to write my lectures and another week to teach at the seminar being held at the University of Dallas.

The effect of that teaching was explosive. All my suppressed intellectual interests burst forth. I was so wired up that I could not sleep for days. By the end of the seminar, the seminar organizer from IHS suggested that maybe it was time for me to switch from practice to teaching. I could not disagree.

So after my third year in the State's Attorney's Office, I decided to seek a position as a law professor. Seeking was easy. Finding, I learned, was not. That meant I had to continue on as an assistant state's attorney for another year. Unfortunately, I'd lost a bit of the single-minded focus, and I began to plan for another run at the teaching market.

In November of 1980, at the same time I was unsuccessfully pursuing an academic position, my boss, Bernard Carey, was running for his third term as state's attorney. A reform-minded Republican in deeply Democratic Cook County, he'd won the office in 1972 as an anti-corruption candidate, defeating the incumbent Democrat, Edward Hanrahan. Race also played a role in Carey's original victory.

Carey carried ten out of fourteen of Chicago's black wards, which since the 1930s had typically been won by Democratic candidates. How did a Republican manage to win a county-wide election for state's attorney, even if he had been a former FBI agent?

In 1969, Hanrahan had organized a raid of the Black Panther Party headquarters by Chicago Police officers, which resulted in the killing of charismatic leader Fred Hampton and another man. (This raid was almost certainly coordinated with, if not ordered by, J. Edgar Hoover's FBI. Hoover was as afraid of Hampton as he had been of Martin Luther King Jr.) The cops claimed that the Panthers had fired first, but photos allegedly showing bullet holes from gunfire directed at them that the cops offered to support their claim of self-defense turned out to be nail heads.

Figure 35. Edward Hanrahan 1968 campaign button

Hanrahan, a tough-talking graduate of Harvard Law and former U.S. Attorney for the Northern District of Illinois, was indicted for obstruction of justice and conspiracy to present false evidence. Although he was acquitted, he'd lost the crucial political support of the African American community, who joined with suburban Republicans to elect Bernie Carey.

For what it's worth, the prosecutors I worked with who had previously worked for Hanrahan, like Kenny Malatesta, thought highly of him.

Once elected, Carey managed the office in a nonpartisan manner. In the past, you might have needed a letter from a Democratic ward committeeman to get a job as an ASA. Indeed, I'd needed such a letter to obtain a summer job as a fee clerk with the Illinois Secretary of State's Office. But I was able to get that job on the strength of a letter from a Republican committeeman because, in 1970, Republican John W. Lewis Jr. had become the secretary of state following the death of his Democratic predecessor, Paul Powell.

In death, Paul Powell became notorious. As the AP reported: "$750,000 in cash, stuffed mostly in attache cases but also in at least one gift box from Marshall Field & Co.," was found "in his suite at Springfield's St. Nicholas Hotel. Another $50,000 was stashed in his Capitol office about five blocks away. A federal investigation concluded Powell skimmed much of it by awarding contracts to friends with kickback conditions. His estate, settled in 1978, was worth $4.6 million, the equivalent of about $21.8 million today. He had $1 million worth of stock in horse tracks where he determined the most favorable racing dates." Even in Chicago, Powell deserved a place in the corruption pantheon. Powell, who never made more than $30,000 as the secretary of state or, before that, as the Speaker of the Illinois House of Representatives, was known to insiders for his saying, "There's only one thing worse than a defeated politician, and that's a broke one."

This scandal allowed a Republican to win the election to replace Powell, which allowed me to get a summer patronage job. My dad had no political connections, but as we were truly Republicans, I asked for a letter from my Republican committeeman and received it. Three years later, a Democrat resumed control of the office.

Had Republican Carey not been the state's attorney, I would likely not have gotten my dream job as an assistant state's attorney. That the office hired based on merit explained why most of my colleagues were law and order Democrats from the working or middle classes. In my years there, I personally saw no political influence being exerted from above.

Carey pledged to investigate and fight voter fraud, political corruption, kickbacks, and other crimes by the Democratic establishment of Chicago and Cook County. He established the Special Prosecutions Bureau for just this purpose, though I can't say it accomplished all that much. Like Ol' Man River, Cook County corruption just kept rolling along, seemingly unstoppable. Still, as I mentioned before, I found the State's Attorney's Office itself to be surprisingly free of corruption, which was important to me.

One of Carey's initiatives to fight voter fraud was election duty. Assistant state's attorneys like me were tasked with patrolling polling stations on Election Day. (Yes, in those days, we had Election Day when everyone voted.) Each of us was accompanied by a Cook County Sheriff's policeman as we went from polling station to polling station to try to detect election fraud in Chicago. It was not a day that any of us relished, not least because it seemed entirely fruitless. Exactly how were we going to catch election fraud by sticking our heads randomly into polling places?

In 1976, four years after defeating Democrat Edward Hanrahan, Carey had won reelection, the first Republican ever to be reelected State's Attorney of Cook County. In November of 1980, he was running for a third term. This time his opponent was Richard "Rich" M. Daley, son of Richard J. Daley, the political boss who had died a month after Carey's reelection.

Rich Daley, the son, had been an influential Illinois state legislator, where he was reputed to throw his political weight around. He was widely called "Richie" by those who resented the arrogance of "Boss" Daley's son. In his bid for Cook County State's Attorney, Rich Daley had his father's powerful machine behind him, with this office presumably being the stepping stone to the mayoralty (which in fact he did achieve nine years later).

On November 4, 1980, I was tasked with election duty. The Cook County Sheriff's policeman assigned to me was a big-talking, macho-type cop. Sheriff's policemen worked for the county, not the city, and in general had a bit of an inferiority complex vis-a-vis Chicago PD officers.

The process of voting was simple. Registered voters filled out a ballot application card, signed their name on the card, and handed the card to the election judges, who then located the voter's registration in a binder containing the voter's signature. If the signature on the application card and the signature on the registration matched, the voter was legitimate. If the signatures didn't match, election fraud had just been attempted.

To perform this task, there were supposed to be both Republican and Democrat election judges at every precinct, but this was a sham. There really aren't enough Republicans in Chicago, and there was little to stop a Democrat from claiming to be a Republican. Consequently, the "Republican" judges were usually Democrats.

Also assigned to every precinct was a uniformed Chicago Police Department officer, whose job was to ensure the security of the polling place.

My job was to spend fifteen to thirty minutes at each precinct before moving on to the next until I'd visited each of my assigned precincts. Having never done election duty before, like Felony Review, this was yet another novel experience beyond that of preparing and trying cases. As far as I knew, none of us had ever caught anyone in the act.

At one precinct, located in a school gym, I did what we had been told to do. I walked behind the table of election judges and looked over their shoulders as they processed ballot applications. Not expecting to find anything untoward, I glanced over the election judge's shoulder. That's when I happened to notice that the signature on the card he'd been handed by the voter didn't remotely match the registration signature in the binder. I looked up at the voter. The young African American man who'd handed the card to the judge was obviously a teenager. Then I looked down at the binder to see that the registered voter was in his sixties.

I had just witnessed attempted election fraud. Now what? I don't believe we were told what to do if this ever happened. So I did the only thing I could think of. I told Patrolman Archibald, the uniformed Chicago police officer assigned to this precinct, to arrest the teen. He asked me why. I said the teen had just committed election fraud.

He looked at me like I was crazy and said, "No, I'm not going to do that." Of course, he and I both knew that an assistant state's attorney was employed by Cook County, not the city of Chicago, and had no authority over him and couldn't compel him to do anything. So I turned to the big-talking Cook County Sheriff's policeman who was tasked with accompanying me and told him to arrest the teen.

Once again, we both knew that I had no authority over him. Even though we were both employed by Cook County, he answered only to the elected Cook County Sheriff, while I answered to the elected state's attorney. He was there primarily as my bodyguard. But maybe, I hoped, he'd do as I asked him and arrest the kid. He said, "No, I don't want to."

The sheriff's cop did at least agree to hold the kid there while I called my supervisor, who would then call his supervisor and let him know what to do. After I placed the call, I was awaiting further instructions when the Democratic precinct captain, also African American, probably about fifty, pulled me aside.

"Can I talk to you?"

"Sure."

"Look," he said, "Don't come down on the kid, I'm just trying to help your boss. Can you go easy and let this thing pass?"

Help my boss? Of course, I knew that this was a Daley machine operation. But there was no point arguing or laughing at the absurdity of his lie.

I said, "Doesn't matter if you asked him. The fact is, he did it." In the meantime, my supervisor had called the deputy sheriff's supervisor, who instructed him to hold the kid until he could be taken into custody by the CPD. Why didn't I have the precinct captain arrested, too? First of all, it would have been his word against mine. Second, he was known to us and wasn't going anywhere. Whether or not to prosecute him would be up to Special Prosecutions, not me.

At the police station, I advised the kid of his rights. As a former Felony Review assistant, interviewing perps was now familiar territory for me. His name was Charles Mitchell, the same name as the registered voter. But he was only seventeen. Charles told me he had been home in bed asleep when he was awakened by a man who told him he could vote because "they got your name." The man gave him a card with a name and address to use. Charles admitted that he knew he was ineligible to vote but would not give the name of the man who brought him to the polling station. But he added, "If I have to go to court, then I'll tell some names."

I swore out the complaint for perjury and forgery as I had been instructed to do by Special Prosecutions. Six days later, in preliminary hearing court, Mitchell pled guilty to forgery in return for a sentence of two years of felony probation. I never learned whether Special Pros elicited his cooperation against the precinct captain in return for the plea deal.

To this day, requiring matching signatures is the most important way to combat voter fraud—especially when voting with mail-in ballots rather than in person, when a picture ID establishes one's identity. Yet there are states where this requirement has been waived. Without that signature-match requirement, there will be no evidence to prove that a mail-in ballot is fraudulent.

* * *

Richard M. Daley prevailed by 16,000 votes out of 2.1 million cast over Bernie Carey—50.39 percent to 49.61 percent. For those of us who prided ourselves on working for a nonpartisan prosecutor, this was like a death sentence. The next day at 26th Street may as well have been a wake. Everyone walked around like numbed zombies. We thought our days were numbered.

Yet that's not how things turned out. As I already mentioned, until that point, "Richie" Daley's reputation as a state legislator in Springfield was as a hot-headed, entitled bully who wielded power on behalf of his dad. Now Rich Daley aspired to be mayor. His ticket to realizing that goal was to do a good job as State's Attorney. And, at least when I was there, he did.

Indeed, in some ways the office improved. All of our supervisors, like Mike Ficaro, resigned to be replaced by Daley's picks. Most of Carey's supervisors were excellent, but a few had risen to their level of incompetence. We expected them all to be replaced by hard-core Democratic partisan hacks. But that's not what happened.

Daley named Richard Devine as 1st Assistant, the man who really called the shots at the office. Devine was a smart, reform-minded Democrat and a graduate of Northwestern Law. I met him and I liked him. I was impressed that he even decided to try some cases himself. And, after Daley became mayor, Devine went on to win election as Cook County State's Attorney in 1996, where he served three terms.

When I left the office to become a research fellow at the University of Chicago in 1981, rather than have me resign, Devine blessed me with a year-long leave of absence in case I did not land a tenure-track teaching job afterwards. Devine was impressed both by my academic aspirations and the fact I was going to be at the University of Chicago.

Of greatest significance to us was that Daley and Devine apparently had good sources of information as to who among the ranks were good, honest prosecutors and who were the politicos. All of his appointments were the good ones. Indeed, one boastful and arrogant Democrat we all feared would be elevated was passed over.

"So I Have to Change My Opinion"

NOT LONG AFTER John Crowley attended my wedding to Beth, something happened behind the scenes to spring him from misdemeanor Siberia to hearing felonies at 26th and California. I don't know what it was, but I was thrilled for him. The office supervisors were no dummies. My friendship with the judge was by then well-known, and I was promoted from 3rd chair in Judge Barbaro's courtroom to 2nd chair in Crowley's.

Figure 36. Judge John Crowley visits my evidence class

My 1st chair there was Joe Locallo, a superb prosecutor with a biting, dry wit. Being assigned to Crowley's courtroom was the best assignment I could've had, given his warm feelings toward me. But Crowley was as demanding a judge as Pincham and even more cantankerous. Plus, he was knowledgeable about the law and its structure: what made sense and what didn't.

Figure 37. John J. Crowley campaign button

There are two moments in my experience as a jury trial lawyer I am most proud of, and both occurred in Judge Crowley's courtroom. The first is how I got a psychiatrist expert witness for the defense to change his opinion on cross-examination. The second concerned a hearsay objection that I decided *not* to make. Both were murder cases. But sandwiched in between these moments of triumph was a moment of weakness when my failure to prepare cost me, as my clinical professor Nick Littlefield had warned me. That, too, was a murder case.

Or at least it should have been.

* * *

According to the Illinois Supreme Court's summary of the events, "Nina Williams, Renee Martin, Debra Johnson, and Lanita Foster were volunteers for a political candidate in the city of Chicago. The four women … left the candidate's campaign headquarters at approximately 1 a.m. … and began walking towards Williams's car, which was parked on a city street. Two men were walking towards the women."

One of the men, Eldrix Arnold, "approached them and asked for a cigarette. Debra Johnson told Arnold they did not have cigarettes." As the women began to get into the car, Arnold pushed his way into the vehicle, pointed a handgun at the back of Nina Williams's head, pulled the trigger, and shot her in the head, killing her. "After Arnold shot Williams, he told the women to 'give up' the money." When Johnson then threw Williams's purse to Arnold, the defendant "caught the purse and ran down the street."

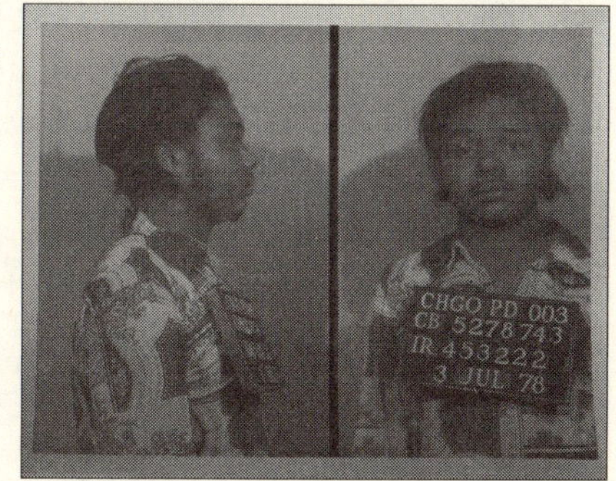

Figure 38. Eldrix Arnold
(courtesy of Chicago Police Department)

In a statement to the police, Arnold claimed that the gun discharge was an accident. At trial, however, his defense was voluntary intoxication. According to the Illinois pattern jury instruction, "An intoxicated person is criminally responsible for his conduct unless his intoxication renders him incapable of acting knowingly [or] intentionally."

A voluntary intoxication defense is similar to an insanity defense because it goes to the responsibility of the accused for his admitted actions. The difference is that, with an insanity defense, the lack of responsibility is due to a mental disease or defect, whereas with voluntary intoxication, the lack of responsibility is due to the voluntary consumption of an intoxicant. Unlike mental disease, which is comparatively rare, people voluntarily get intoxicated all the time. Therefore, the law is very skeptical about voluntary intoxication as a defense. You have to be incredibly wasted.

To support their theory that the defendant was so intoxicated that he was "incapable of acting knowingly or intentionally," the defense had the defendant examined by psychiatrist Don W. Sellers, director of the Lutheran Alcohol Treatment Center in Park Ridge, Illinois. In his report to the public defenders, Sellers did not offer a final opinion on whether Arnold was responsible for his actions. But I knew that was the opinion for which he was being called to testify.

Most psychiatrists who testify for the defense are professional witnesses, commonly referred to as "hired guns." They're called forensic psychiatrists. Unlike clinical psychiatrists who regularly see patients, they typically earn their living by testifying in court. Sometimes they spend no more than an hour with the defendant, and sometimes not even that; they might only peruse the file. You pay them, they testify. The prosecutors had their own hired guns who worked for the state-run Chicago-Read Mental Health Center. Don Sellers, however, was a real psychiatrist with a real practice and real patients, and his specialty was alcoholism.

In February of 1981, the murder trial of Eldrix Arnold was held before Judge Crowley. After the prosecution rested, it was time for the defense case. The public defenders told Dr. Sellers to be at court at ten in the morning, seating him in a witness room located next to the judge's chambers. There he sat as the court went about its daily business before the trial resumed. And he sat. And sat some more. All alone.

I walked past the open door of the witness room numerous times as I handled the morning call and could see him sitting there. Finally, I stuck my head in the doorway and asked whether I could get him anything—maybe coffee or a drink. He said coffee would be nice. I fetched him a cup, and when I handed it to him, I thought I could detect how irritated he was becoming at the wait. I might have been wrong about that, but I knew he was testifying pro bono, meaning he wasn't receiving his hourly charge times however many hours he'd already been there before even testifying. This was a busy professional who was being taken away from his many responsibilities.

From his report, I already knew what he was going to say on the stand, and my planned line of questioning was based on that. However, on the spur of the moment, I sat down and said, "I am the prosecutor for the case you are going to testify in. Do you mind talking with me?"

There was nothing improper about this. Defense attorneys are allowed to interview prosecution witnesses, and prosecutors are allowed to interview defense witnesses to prepare lines of questioning and possible rebuttals. But I decided to do something that, while entirely proper, was highly unusual. I revealed to this expert witness for the defense my line of cross-examination. It sounds crazy, but I had a good reason.

Psychiatrists who have not actually treated a defendant render their expert opinion on the defendant's mental state based on their examination, cursory or not, and a hypothetical question containing the facts that will have been presented to the jury by other witnesses. After being asked to assume a sometimes-long list of facts, they are then asked whether they have an expert opinion about the hypothetical defendant's mental state. During its deliberations, the jury will then decide for itself whether the evidence presented to it showed that the actual defendant sufficiently resembled the hypothetical defendant the expert expressed his opinion about.

During cross-examination, a prosecutor will typically ask his own hypothetical question with facts from the testimony of other witnesses that the defense had omitted from theirs. That was what I was prepared to do.

"Just so you're not surprised on the witness stand," I explained, "here are the questions I intend to ask you." I then identified all the facts we had proved as "hypothetical" facts on which I would ask him to base his opinion of the defendant's mental state. But I did not ask him what his ultimate expert opinion of the defendant's mental state would be on the basis of these hypothetical facts. I left that for the courtroom.

The objective of this line of cross-examination is not to get the expert to change his opinion on cross. It is to make his opinion seem incredible to the jury when he sticks to his original opinion notwithstanding the additional hypothetical facts I was going to include—all of which were based on the evidence we had presented to the jury showing the actual facts of the case.

Here, I decided to reveal to Dr. Sellers all the hypothetical facts I would ask him to assume were true so he would have time to think about how he would respond when asked the ultimate question. I figured if there was any chance at all for him to change his expert opinion—to which his written report did not commit him—it would not be in the heat of cross-examination in front of a jury after these hypothetical facts were sprung on him for the first time. He would need a little time to mull over the answer he would want to give. Whether or not he changed his mind, I was prepared for whatever he was going to say on the stand.

I then left him alone. When the trial resumed and another couple of witnesses had testified, the defense called Dr. Sellers to the stand. As expected, the defense attorney established the doctor's impressive credentials before leading him through a long recitation based on a hypothetical defendant with the identical biography and facts of the actual defendant: crappy childhood, alcoholic since age thirteen, abuser of drugs, too, a history of being hospitalized for acute alcohol poisoning, and on the day of the crime had drunk wine and spirits for several hours before committing the act.

Then came the defense attorney's money question:

"I would ask you further, Doctor, again, based on your expertise and the facts that I have just related to you, do you have an opinion to a reasonable degree of medical certainty as to whether that intoxication would render this hypothetical man incapable of acting knowingly or intentionally?"

"It's my opinion," the doctor answered, "that he would not be able to act knowingly or intentionally."

Now it was my turn. I began by trying to elicit from the doctor his impressions of the defendant when they met eight months after the incident, and I probed whether the defendant had said anything that might cause the doctor to question whether he was being entirely truthful about not being able to remember the moment of the crime. Here, I was consciously trying to emulate the line of cross that I'd seen Ron Guzmán use in Judge Pincham's court that had so impressed me.

The defense objected strenuously to the line of questioning, and the back and forth led to the jury being taken out of the room while we hashed out how far I'd be allowed to take my questioning. The hashing took quite a while before it resolved mostly in my favor, and the jury was led back in.

"Well," the doctor said, "I felt that he was exaggerating some of the memory lapses and his alcohol intake. He seemed to have a very good recollection as to how much he had been drinking over the period of time prior to the incident. And then by the way he slanted it in his favor, I felt that he was protecting himself."

I'd known what that answer was going to be, because it was in his report.

Now it was time to present my own hypothetical that I'd prepared the doctor to expect.

"I'd like you to assume, Doctor, that approximately one and a half hours before the shooting incident the hypothetical man in question walked his girlfriend and his daughter to the girlfriend's mother's house a distance of about three blocks in cold weather and slippery conditions, and that this hypothetical man, while doing so, never fell down. I'd like you to further assume that before the hypothetical man left his apartment, he left some of his money in the apartment in the amount of fifteen dollars, and he took twenty dollars with him at the time, and that he remembers the twenty dollars that he took with him to consist of ten singles and a ten-dollar bill."

And so it went for many minutes, with the hypothetical man dropping off his girlfriend at her apartment before going to his mother's apartment and letting himself in with one of the keys on his key ring, then playing records on her phonograph, then grabbing a handgun owned by his mother and putting it in a paper bag, then walking to a liquor store that was closed and having to find another that was open before tucking the gun into his waistband beneath his shirt and jacket, and going into a bar where he saw a woman who offered him a sip of her drink, which he remembered to be rum and Coke, then buying some wine at the bar and paying with his ten-dollar bill the exact amount of $8.80, which he remembered, then leaving the bar and asking some girls who were outside on the street if they had a cigarette—all of that within seventy-five minutes before the crime.

"Doctor, do you have an opinion, based upon a reasonable degree of medical certainty, whether at that time that that hypothetical man was able to act knowingly and intentionally?"

"From your description," he said, "I would have to say that he was able to act knowingly and intentionally."

At that point, a few of the jurors could not suppress their laughter. After this, I resumed my cross-examination with still more hypothetical facts about the defendant, which Joe and I had proved during the trial.

"Assuming all those facts, do you have an opinion based upon a reasonable degree of medical certainty as to whether this hypothetical man was able to act intentionally or knowingly at the time of the shooting?"

"Yes."

"What is the opinion?"

"That he was able to act knowingly and intentionally. *So I have to change my opinion.*"

"Thank you, Doctor. I have no further questions."

At that moment, the trial was won. Of course, the jury voted to convict. But this didn't end the case. At the end of any trial, the judge instructs the jury on the law. The Illinois Supreme Court publishes patterned jury instructions on all the issues that typically arise during a trial. Most trial judges will never deviate from the safe harbor of these instructions. But Judge Crowley was not most judges.

The defense asked the judge to give the patterned jury instruction for voluntary intoxication, which I quoted above. Judge Crowley denied the motion on the grounds that the evidence would not support a reasonable jury in finding that the standard for voluntary manslaughter had been met. On appeal, the Illinois Court of Appeals reversed the conviction, but sometime later, the Illinois Supreme Court reversed the Court of Appeals and restored the conviction. "A trial judge has the discretion to refuse to tender a defense instruction on intoxication where there is insufficient evidence for a jury to reasonably find that the defendant was so intoxicated at the time of the crime that he lacked the requisite mental state for the crime," wrote Justice Clark for the court. After a long recital of the evidence that I summarized in my hypothetical to the doctor, Justice Clark then referred to my cross-examination.

> The most significant testimony, however, was from the defendant's expert. … [D]uring cross-examination, the State asked the defendant's expert to assume the facts given during direct examination plus additional facts of the defendant's activities before, during and immediately after the shooting. With these additional facts, the following exchange took place:
>
> "Q. Assuming all those facts, do you have an opinion

> based upon a reasonable degree of medical certainty as to whether this hypothetical man was able to act intentionally or knowingly at the time of the shooting?
>
> A. Yes.
>
> Q. What is the opinion?
>
> A. That he was able to act knowingly and intelligently [sic]. So I had [sic] to change my opinion."

Justice Clark then concluded: "The opinion of the defendant's expert, plus the coherent and detailed nature of the defendant's memory, 'clearly indicate that the defendant had a cognizance of the events immediately prior to the shooting which belies any arguments that his power of reasoning had been suspended.' … We therefore conclude that the trial judge properly instructed the jury at the conclusion of the trial."

Winning a trial is not enough. To sustain a conviction, one must also win on appeal. What I did here helped assure that later success. Getting an expert witness to change his opinion on cross was one of the two highlights of my jury trial experience.

In another jury trial, a dispute over jury instructions did not go as well.

"I Know What I Think It Says. Now You Tell Me What You Think It Says"

ON JULY 11, 1980, Keith Hoddenbach—a.k.a. "Popeye"—shot and killed Orlando Roman.

Hoddenbach claimed that he had received a threatening message from Roman, who was a rival gang member. Hoddenbach went to his girlfriend's house, where he retrieved his fully loaded .38 revolver, then drove to 2015 North Damen Avenue, where he "saw Roman on the steps with about nine people." Roman walked to the car after Hoddenbach called him over. The two men "talked for about five minutes." Hoddenbach claimed he asked Roman to forget their previous dispute, and that Roman replied that "he would rather kill the defendant," at which point he "pulled up" a gun. Claiming that "he thought Roman intended to murder him," Hoddenbach grabbed his gun from his car, shot Roman, and fled the scene. Hoddenbach was arrested and charged with murder.

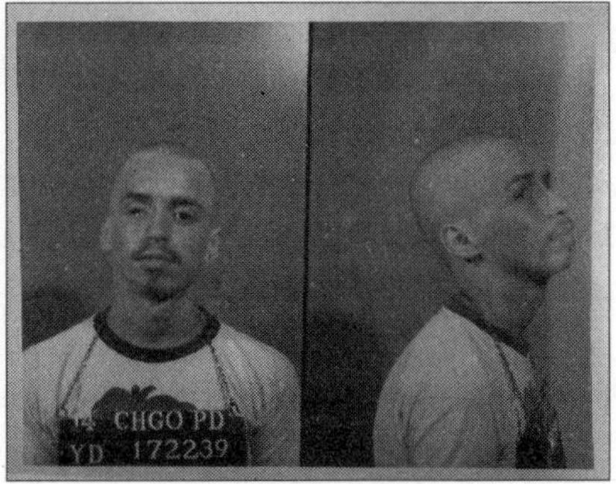

Figure 39. Keith Hoddenbach
(courtesy of Chicago Police Department)

At the conclusion of Hoddenbach's trial, in addition to a self-defense instruction, the defense also asked the jury to be instructed on voluntary manslaughter. My partner and I opposed the motion. If the jury bought the defendant's self-defense story, they would acquit. But if they rejected self-defense, we contended that there was little or nothing to support the voluntary manslaughter charge.

A conviction for murder carried with it a minimum penalty of twenty years in the penitentiary—with the potential of being reduced by half for good behavior. The maximum penalty for voluntary manslaughter was just six years' incarceration, reducible to three after good time. Given that both Hoddenbach and Roman were gang members, we did not want the jury to compromise on the lesser charge. We wanted them to have to choose between murder and acquittal, in which case we thought they'd convict Hoddenbach of murder.

The 1st chair in the case was Jack Smeeton, who was handling the case from charging to trial as a member of the Gang Special Prosecution Unit. In the late '60s, Jack had played running back for the Northwestern Wildcats football team. I was his 2nd chair in the trial.

The defense attorney was Mark Solock, a DePaul law graduate and a public defender on the Murder Task Force. The Murder Task Force was a premier unit within the Cook County Public Defender's Office. There was a saying among criminals when offered the representation of a public defender: "I don't want a public defender. I want a real lawyer." However generally unfair that was to public defenders (PDs), in the case of the PDs on the Murder Task Force, it was dead wrong. The Task Force lawyers were excellent. Unlike regular PDs (and ASAs) who were assigned to the courtrooms of particular judges, Murder Task Force attorneys were assigned to particular defendants, handling their cases from bond court to trial and sentencing.

When I was summer clerking in Judge Machala's courtroom, several Murder Task Force lawyers lobbied me to become a PD rather than an ASA. Had I been guaranteed a spot on the Murder Task Force, I might have taken that option more seriously. After all, it was the TV show *The Defenders* that inspired me to be a lawyer. But the Cook County Public Defender's Office was notoriously political, which was par for the course for every unit of government in Cook County other than the State's Attorney's Office. Even if I could get a job as a PD, there was no telling whether I could rise to become a member of the Task Force.

With a couple of exceptions, I always respected the public defenders with whom I worked. Like criminal defense attorneys generally, public defenders perform an essential role in the criminal justice system. By holding the prosecutors to their burden of proof in every case, they protected the innocent from being charged in the first place. That was what the Felony Review Unit was all about: anticipating how a good defense attorney would deconstruct a case, and refusing to charge where the evidence was insufficient to prove a case beyond a reasonable doubt. No defense attorney, no Felony Review. No Felony Review, far more innocent people wrongly prosecuted for crimes they did not commit.

My respect for public defenders also proved to be professionally beneficial to me. When I was being considered for a job as a law professor at the Chicago-Kent College of Law, one of the faculty members there, Shelvin Singer, was a former PD. Before he could support my candidacy, he checked with his contacts at the PD's office to see how I had treated PDs when I was an ASA. "Tough but fair" was their reply. When Shelvin told me that story after I joined the faculty, I was genuinely proud that this was my reputation among PDs. I was also retroactively relieved. The idea that a prosecutor's future career was in any way in the hands of a public defender was a little terrifying.

While I strived to treat all PDs with respect, I especially respected members of the Murder Task Force. Attorneys like Mark Solock, whom I found to be particularly sharp in all his trial skills, were the reason why. When we objected to Solock's motion for a voluntary manslaughter instruction, he replied that there was an appellate court decision that justified a voluntary manslaughter instruction on facts like these.

After our objection, Judge Crowley broke his courtroom for lunch. I went back to my office and worked on whatever still needed doing. What I didn't do was read the case that Solock had cited. As I recall, he did not provide the case name, and I would have had to hunt for it. But I didn't do any research of my own on the question.

To be frank, by then, I'd become highly skeptical of any defense citations to cases and, as a result, overly complacent. Throughout my time as a prosecutor, I'd heard defense attorneys make motions based on this case or that case. I got so used to them misstating what the case law said that I began automatically assuming that any citation to a case that did not make sense to me either said the opposite of what the lawyer claimed it did or had nothing at all to do with the facts of the case at hand. Time and again, when I asked the attorney to show me the case he was citing, I could immediately spot why it didn't really say what the attorney represented it to say.

This tendency was brought to the fore by the rise of ChatGPT, which has become notorious in the legal world for providing attorneys with case law that not only fails to support the argument they're making, but doesn't exist at all. According to *The Washington Post*: "Courts across the country are facing a deluge of filings from attorneys and litigants that back their arguments with nonexistent research hallucinated by generative artificial intelligence, prompting judges to fight back with fines and reprimands." One researcher cited by the *Post* "said he's found 95 such instances in the United States since June 2023 — including 58 this year. They include cases where attorneys or other participants admitted to using AI in filings that contained errors, or judges reported references to nonexistent cases or quotations. 'It has been accelerating.'"

The *Post* detailed just some of the many lawyers who have been sanctioned for providing nonexistent or misleading citations. These lawyers hadn't even bothered to verify that the cases ChatGPT had provided them were real, much less read the opinions to see if they supported the legal conclusion for which they were being cited. This slovenliness about case citations had been my consistent experience as a prosecutor, which led to a bit of slovenliness of my own. I neither bothered to verify Solock's citation nor found any cases to the contrary.

After lunch, I went into the judge's chambers. Judge Crowley was sitting behind his desk, reading an open volume of the Illinois appellate reporter. I said, "What've you got there, Judge?" He told me it was the case cited by the defense attorney.

I asked what it said.

Just as he had in misdemeanor branch court—when he'd throw the file down on the bench and say, "Mr. State's Attorney! What're you gonna do about this?"—Crowley grabbed the open book by its spine, turned it so it was now facing me, and then slammed it on his desk. Looking me straight in the eyes, he barked, "Well, I know what I think it says. Now you tell me what you think it says."

"Let me take a look," I said.

Oops. The defense attorney had accurately cited this case. Given that I had done no independent research of my own, I had no choice but to say, "Looks like we're going to have to do it his way."

Judge Crowley instructed the jury that they could consider voluntary manslaughter as a lesser-included offense, and that's what they came back with. So what was charged as a murder case ended up as guilty of voluntary manslaughter. Judge Crowley sentenced him to the maximum of six years in the penitentiary.

Moral of the story? Never get complacent. As Nick Littlefield warned me, always be prepared. Had that case been limited or reversed? Were there other appellate cases that went the other way? I will never know because I didn't look when I had the chance. Perhaps the defense attorney was completely right about the law, in which case my failure to do any research was what appellate courts call "harmless error." It is possible. But due to my skepticism about defense attorneys' citations, I will never be sure of this, and I will always regret my failure to look. A verdict of guilty for voluntary manslaughter, however, was still a *G*. So my jury trial record remained intact.

Not in My House

ANTHONY HALL WAS charged with attempted rape, armed robbery, and aggravated kidnapping. The rape was only "attempted" because he was unable to sustain an erection during the attack. As summarized by the court of appeals, Hall had assaulted the victim on the street "by putting his arm around her and brandishing a knife. Despite her attempts to resist, he forcibly led her to a vacant lot and then to a concealed back stairway of an apartment building."

The defendant then "demanded money and forced her to sit on the stairs, instructing her to lower her pants. As she attempted to stall for time, he removed the knife from his pants and placed it on the stairs." The victim then tried to get control of the knife. "In a struggle for the knife," the victim "sustained cuts to her hand. Following this, he physically assaulted her, pulled down her hat to obscure her vision, and then attempted sexual assault while holding the knife. Although he did not complete the act, he proceeded to rob her of money and her gold chain, which she pleaded with him to leave due to its sentimental value. After taking her belongings, he briefly left but returned to take the gold chain before finally departing."

Hall was captured after a foot chase by officers, who found him hiding in a stairwell. The arresting officers told me that he had defecated in his pants. (That info came by way of their warning me not to open the evidence bag containing his clothing.) Hall had previously been imprisoned and had been the object of repeated sexual assaults while there, which may have explained both his inability to perform sexually, as well as his failure to control his bowels, and perhaps also his desire to rape others.

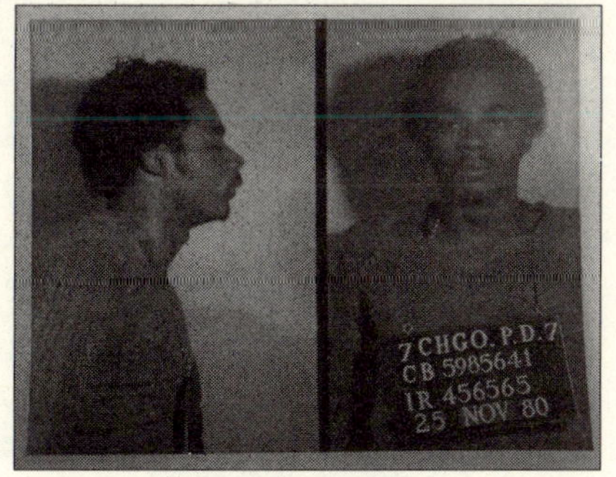

Figure 40. Anthony Hall
(courtesy of Chicago Police Department)

During the trial, a tall, heavyset black man who had been in the courtroom began to follow me and the victim, who was also black, as I escorted her from my office in the office building tower up the elevator to the courtroom. In the elevator, he stood directly next to the victim and physically loomed over her, and me as well.

When I returned to the courtroom, I informed Judge Crowley of what had happened. He asked me what I wanted him to do about it. I said I would like him to call the man into his chambers with a court reporter so we could get his identity on the record. He agreed and, when we did so, it turned out that the man was the cousin of the defendant. Because he was on the defense list of witnesses (as an alibi witness), I then moved that he be excluded from the courtroom, which was entirely normal. He would later testify before the jury.

After the jury returned a verdict of guilty on all counts, they were escorted by bailiffs to their cars in the parking structure on the other side of 26th Street from the courthouse. The next day, several jurors called to tell me that, as they drove out of the structure, they saw the defendant's cousin writing down their plate numbers and pointing at them with his pen as he did. They knew who the person was, of course, because they'd seen him testify, and they felt threatened. I thought the cousin was basically a blowhard and they had nothing to worry about. But having asked the jury to do their duty and convict the defendant, I felt I owed it to them to do what I could about this.

My first move was to go to my supervisors to see if they would approve a felony charge of intimidating a juror. But after hearing about the pen pointing, they understandably declined. Undeterred, I returned to my office and looked at my copy of Chapter 38, the paperback edition of the Illinois criminal code we were charged with enforcing.

Underneath the felony of juror intimidation, I saw there was a misdemeanor offense of "communicating with a juror" as a result of their jury service. Because it was a misdemeanor, I did not need a supervisor's approval to bring that charge, but how to do it? In a very routinized criminal justice system, there was no procedure for such a thing.

I decided to go to Judge Gino DiVito, who was then sitting in a preliminary hearing court in the 26th Street Criminal Court Building. Gino had known me since I was a law student clerk, and he was the head of the Criminal Division of the State's Attorney's Office. He was now a circuit court judge.

I informed Judge DiVito of what happened and swore out a complaint

I had drafted against the cousin. I then asked him to issue a bench warrant for his arrest, which he did. What now? Again, there was no procedure for enforcing a warrant like this one. As far as the legal system was concerned, it was just a piece of paper.

I left telephone messages for the "warrant officer" in the Chicago Police Department district police station in which the cousin resided. Warrant officers are supposed to serve warrants, but they had a reputation for being notoriously lazy. This particular warrant officer neither took any action nor returned my calls. So I escalated.

When Chicago police officers testified in court, they were entitled to time off from their regular duties as compensation for the time spent in court. State's attorneys would sign "time due slips" for the amount of time the officers had spent testifying and being prepared to testify, which would then be cashed in by the officer to get their paid time off the job.

I got the district commander on the phone. I told him about the warrant that had been issued for the cousin, and how the warrant officer had done nothing about it. I then promised a *week's* worth of time due slips to any cop who would arrest him. In essence, I was bribing the district cops to get them to do their job. Within hours, the cousin was in custody. (A few days later, the arresting officers came to my office at 26th and Cal to collect their time due slips.)

I appeared in the misdemeanor branch court in which the cousin—now a defendant himself—was being arraigned. I knew from my days in misdemeanor branch courts that the inexperienced ASAs there would have no idea what this was all about. As a felony trial prosecutor, I could command their respect.

Speaking to the defendant in court, I still pegged him as a blowhard. He had a decent job—in the music business, as I recall—and was not a bad guy. I instructed the ASA there to plead the case to a year's supervision. Supervision was a preliminary conviction that could be expunged from the defendant's record if he wasn't convicted of some other crime within the period of supervision. This was pretty much the least serious penalty the cousin could have faced.

But I had made my point. If I were on the cousin's turf, I would know to play by its rules. Well, the courthouse was *my* turf, and he needed to know that on *my* turf, in *my* house, what he did was out of bounds.

His cousin Anthony Hall was sentenced by Judge Crowley to forty years in the penitentiary for armed robbery and armed violence.

Attorneys' Tricks

IN JUNE OF 1981, not quite four years after becoming an assistant state's attorney, I was promoted to 1st chair in a felony courtroom at 26th and California. The management of a courtroom was now in my hands. I would get to decide who tried which case. I would make the plea bargain decisions. My 2nd chair was John Feely, and my 3rd chair was Paul Tsukuno.

The presiding judge in the courtroom to which I was assigned was the Honorable Leonard R. Grazian. Born in 1924, Grazian was a graduate of John Marshall Law School. He was a cheerful, heavyset Jewish man who walked with a pronounced limp—the result of wounds he had received in combat in World War II. (He died in 2017 and is buried at Arlington National Cemetery, where my dad is also interred.)

Figure 41. Judge Leonard Grazian

Judge Grazian also happened to have been my father's boyhood friend and business attorney. "Lenny"—as he was known in my family—was very fond of me, and I of him. By this time, I had arranged my position as a research fellow at the University of Chicago, which started its fall session at the end of September. So I knew this was to be my last courtroom assignment, and I could not have been happier with it. I'm pretty sure this fortuitous assignment was a complete coincidence. While my supervisors had assigned me to Judge Crowley's courtroom because they were aware of the good relationship I had with him when he was a misdemeanor court judge, they knew nothing of my ties to Lenny Grazian—just as they'd not known of my connection with Eugene Pincham. I just lucked out once again. Which reminds me of another expression from my days as an ASA: "It's not what you know, it's who you know."

I had three jury trials in front of Judge Grazian. The first was a murder case, which I tried with John Feely in July of 1981.

Joel Gunther and Katherine Everett were sleeping on mattresses in a vacant building on Sheridan Road on Chicago's North Side. The building was immediately adjacent to the elevated platform of the Wilson Avenue CTA train station. The two were awakened from their sleep by a man wielding a piece of lumber. The man beat both of them with the board, putting Gunther into a coma from which he would not recover. Katherine survived the attack.

The defendant, Billy Clark, a homeless man who lived in the same vacant building, was identified by Katherine and by CTA maintenance employees who were on the train platform. They heard Katherine's screams, saw Clark beating Gunther on the ground, and called the police. Clark denied being the killer, so the case was one that involved eyewitness testimony.

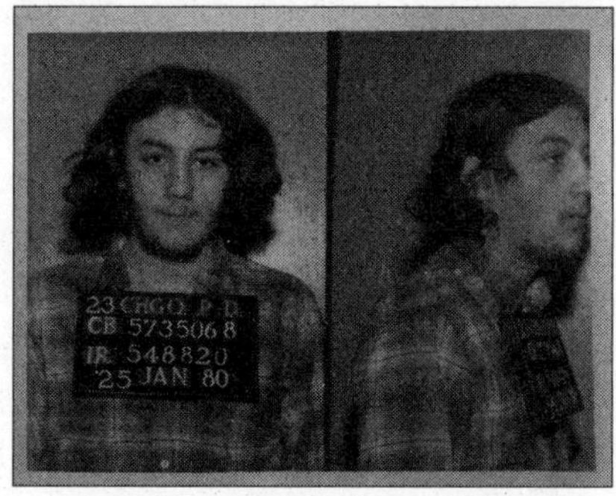

Figure 42. Billy Clark,
(courtesy of Chicago Police Department)

The defendant was represented by the two public defenders assigned to Judge Grazian's courtroom. Having seen their tactics in a previous trial, and being confident that they would engage in similar tactics during this trial, I made the fateful decision to put the jury on notice of what to expect from them in my opening statement. I thought my forewarning would bolster my credibility during closing arguments when I criticized whatever they may have done during the trial to mislead the jury:

> It is like thinking of it in terms of sleight of hand. How does the sleight of hand trick work? It works by getting you to take your eyes off the subject that you are supposed to be looking at and look at some distraction.
>
> *(Objection overruled.)*
>
> … And if you take your eye off the coin and off the evidence in this case and go chasing after what the lawyers tell you, you are going to be in serious trouble. … [W]hen lawyers ask questions of witnesses, sometimes the form of those questions seem to

> indicate that the lawyers may know something about the witness or the facts of the case that you haven't heard in evidence. So if the lawyer asks the question, when did you stop beating your wife. …

At this point, Judge Grazian sustained defense counsel's objection and admonished me to "get into the evidence," which I did.

During the trial, the defense attorneys did as I predicted. When cross-examining Katherine, they suggested that the photographs they were holding contradicted her testimony, which they did not. They knew that these photographs would not be "published" to the jury until much later in the proceeding. But at that point, her testimony had already made a negative impression. (In hindsight, I might have asked the judge to publish the pictures then and there, but that thought never occurred to me.)

In my closing argument, I made reference to these tactics:

> Ladies and gentlemen, you remember the first day of this trial I stood before you. … And I was in the process of telling you the tactics the defense attorney will employ during the trial so you can anticipate that happening … when I was cut short by an objection by the defense.
>
> *(Objection overruled.)*
>
> Well, what I was telling you about was how defense attorneys use sleight of hand in defending people and I can understand why the defense wouldn't want me to tell you about this.
>
> *(Objection overruled.)*
>
> … And what I was in the process of telling you, when you are defending somebody, when you are defending a case where the evidence is as overwhelming as the evidence in this case, there is only one thing you can do—[that] is get the jury to ignore the evidence. … And it is just like a magician uses sleight of hand, the way they make a coin disappear is by

> getting you to look at something else.
>
> The old trick, look at the hand, don't look at the evidence, and that's exactly the way defense attorneys make the evidence disappear by getting you to look at something else and the only something else that is available to them is naked speculation.

I then described what they had done with the photograph as well as how they attempted to "dirty the victim" in an effort to discredit her testimony. "We are subject to these types of tactics, and jurors like yourselves let people like Bobby [sic] Clark go free."

The jury was sent to deliberate. Grazian called me into his chambers. As I stood before him, he delivered a loud and stern reproach. "Don't you ever," he said, "*ever* impugn the integrity of the legal profession like that."

I felt bad about his disapproval, but not too bad, and Clark was convicted. Judge Grazian sentenced him to forty years in the penitentiary. But two years later, the conviction was reversed on appeal due to my closing argument.

* * *

For years, the Illinois Court of Appeals had been warning state's attorneys about their closing arguments. Despite these warnings, such arguments were usually held to be "harmless error" in the face of the evidence of guilt introduced at trial. Or they were deemed to be "invited comment"—that is, an otherwise improper comment that had been instigated by something the defense attorney had said in his or her argument and was therefore permissible. As a result, many ASAs felt no compunction about saying whatever they felt they needed to say to get a conviction, whether it was proper or not.

I was not one of these. I never knowingly made an improper argument and did not knowingly do so in the Billy Clark case. Perhaps to my discredit, I was honestly unaware that my remarks about the defense attorney were improper, or I would not have made them.

But in April of 1983, the Court of Appeals decided to hit the Cook County State's Attorney's Office upside its head. To send its message, it reversed four cases on the same day for improper closing arguments, including mine. I don't think it was a coincidence that none of the cases the court reversed were high-profile. But the message was received loud and clear.

The State's Attorney's Office held a series of training sessions on proper closing arguments for all its prosecutors. At the heart of the training were the four reversed cases. Given that I was a Harvard Law grad, and now a law professor, unsurprisingly, mine in particular drew the usual State's Attorney's ball-busting humor. The joke was that I was the only assistant state's attorney ever to be reversed for an improper opening statement! Of course, this wasn't entirely accurate. The court cited my opening statement as evidence of my "mens rea" or bad intent, and to rebut any claim that my closing argument had been "invited" by something the defense attorney had said in his closing argument. But I can't help but appreciate the humor.

After remanding the case for a new trial, it was plea-bargained to a lower sentence because the maximum the defendant might receive was the forty years to which Judge Grazian had already sentenced him. So that was where the bargaining began. For there to be an incentive to plead guilty, the plea deal had to be for less than forty years (which is really twenty years if the convict is well behaved). I was never informed of the final resolution or what exactly went into the plea negotiation. But the story does not end here.

At the time of the reversals, I was finishing my first year of teaching at the Chicago-Kent College of Law. I taught a two-semester Contracts class to the first-year evening students and a section of the day students. My relationship with the day students was rocky. In the midst of it all, the Chicago newspapers gave the reversals front-page coverage and listed the names of all the prosecutors involved. I knew I would have to say something to the students about it. Sure enough, one of the students had circulated the story to the entire class. When I walked into the classroom, it was unusually quiet, and I could feel all their eyes on me.

I did not defend or attempt to justify my conduct. Instead, I took the opportunity to explain to them exactly *why* my remarks had been improper. The jury is supposed to be focused on the facts and evidence in the case concerning the defendant's guilt. An argument of the kind I made would have the likely effect of shifting the jury's attention away from the defendant's guilt and toward the "guilt" of the defense attorneys, which isn't what juries should be thinking about. That simple, honest explanation relieved all the tension in the room, and we moved on to discussing whatever contract law subject was on the agenda.

But that didn't yet put the issue behind me. Rob Warden was editor and publisher of *Chicago Lawyer*, a publication covering the legal system in Chicago. He decided to write a story on "prosecutorial misconduct" as evidenced by the four reversals. I agreed to the interview. He began by asking me whether I thought there needed to be some method of subjecting such misconduct to independent scrutiny. I told him this was a type of "crime" that takes place in the presence of a police officer, meaning right in front of an independent magistrate: the trial judge. It is up to the trial judge to address and correct this misconduct on the spot. Nothing a review board could do afterwards is likely to be as effective as what is supposed to happen at the very moment the crime occurs. (Rob was so impressed by the thoughtfulness of my interview that, in 1993, he recommended me to the producers of the *Ricki Lake Show* for an episode on persons wrongfully convicted of crime. I tell the story of my appearance on that program in *A Life for Liberty*.)

To this day, I kick myself when remembering my screwup in the Billy Clark case—as I do with the Keith Hoddenbach case. And yet, all it would have taken to have avoided the reversal of Billy Clark's conviction was for Judge Grazian to have *sustained*, rather than overruled, the first defense objection to my closing argument. I would then have moved off the subject. That would have been far preferable to allowing me to continue making the improper argument and then chewing me out in chambers.

One has to assume that, while he really did not like what he thought was my disparagement of the legal profession, he did not realize that my argument was improper. Which made two of us.

"Did You Date Her?"

MY SECOND JURY trial in front of Judge Grazian was an armed robbery case that was unremarkable except for one thing. During jury selection, a "venire," or group of prospective jurors, was brought up from the jury room. From this group would be selected the panel of twelve jurors and two alternates. In those days, each side had ten peremptory challenges they could use to bounce any juror they pleased without cause.

At the beginning, the trial judge asks a series of questions of the venire to identify potential issues that might lead a juror to be removed for cause. The judge asks the lawyers and the defendant to stand and face the jurors in the spectators' section of the courtroom. He then reads the names of the lawyers and the defendant and asks if any of the potential jurors know the defendant or any of the lawyers. In this newly remodeled courtroom, the spectators' seating was separated by a glass partition from the main courtroom, so I could not see any of the venire, though they could see me.

As I took my seat at counsel table, Judge Grazian asked one of the jurors who had raised her hand to enter the main courtroom so he could inquire about the connection. As she stood in the aisle directly next to me, he asked her name. "Carol Wilmowski," she replied. Then, looking down at me, she whispered under her breath, "Carol Brabham."

"I know the prosecutor," she told the judge. Indeed, she did.

Carol Brabham and I had been classmates in grade school, junior high, and high school. We'd never been particularly close, but we were in the same classes at Hoover Grade School and at Schrum Junior High.

After identifying herself, Carol then returned to her seat, and jury selection continued. By the time she was called to the jury box to be examined, the public defenders had exhausted all their peremptory challenges, which is something you try never to do. During their examination of Carol, she disclosed that, not only was she a paralegal who had formerly worked for the U.S. Attorney's Office as a secretary, she was also married to an FBI agent.

The defense attorneys—the same two that I had tried the Billy Clark case against just a week earlier—asked to approach the bench, where they moved that she be dismissed "for cause" on the ground that she had been my classmate. The judge asked me if I had been close to her. "Did you date her?" he asked. I had not. He then asked if I had any objection to her dismissal for cause. I replied that I was in an awkward position and would leave the matter up to him. But I added that the real reason for this "for cause" objection was that the defense attorneys had used up their preemptory challenges, and now learned her husband was in the FBI.

The judge overruled the objection and allowed Carol to remain on the jury. Although I was initially pleased by the ruling, throughout the rest of the trial I became mildly tormented by the possibility that she may not have liked me when we were students. I racked my brain for any recollection of any unpleasantness between us, but could think of none. My main memory of her from our school days together was that she was really cute.

As it happened, the jury deliberated for a long time before returning a guilty verdict. Carol and I spoke on the phone after the case was over. She told me it was she who had held out the jury for so long, because she was concerned about appearances.

* * *

I had other jury trials, of course, each of which was interesting in its own way.

- Michael Hernandez: The defendant grabbed a woman off North State Parkway, pulled her into a stairwell, and raped her. She initially told the police and testified at preliminary hearing that no penetration had occurred, which made it an attempted rape. The victim was a middle-age white Northern European immigrant with a bit of an accent. While I was preparing her to testify, she admitted to me that there had been penetration, but because her attacker was black, she had been too ashamed to admit it to the police. I had to decide whether to

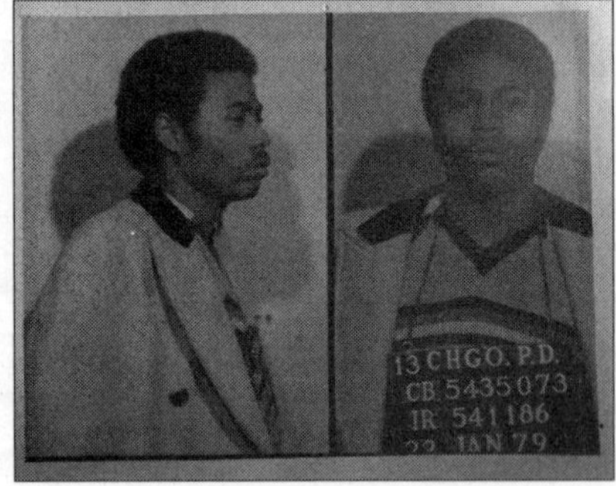

Figure 43. Michael Hernandez
(courtesy of Chicago Police Department)

potentially undermine her credibility as a witness by filing a new count for rape. I decided—as Alice Richmond had advised me when I interned for her in the Suffolk County DA's Office—that honesty was the best policy. I personally went to the grand jury to indict the defendant for rape. We explained the change in her story to the jury during her direct testimony. Guilty of rape and robbery. Sentence: eight years.

- Jose Garcia Huerte and Cresenciano Sanchez. The pair abducted the victim off the street and drove across the state line to Indiana, very near the Route 30 Drive-In Theater I used to take my dates to in high school. We showed that they actually crossed back into Illinois before parking their car and repeatedly raping the victim. Both guilty of rape. Sentence: ten years.

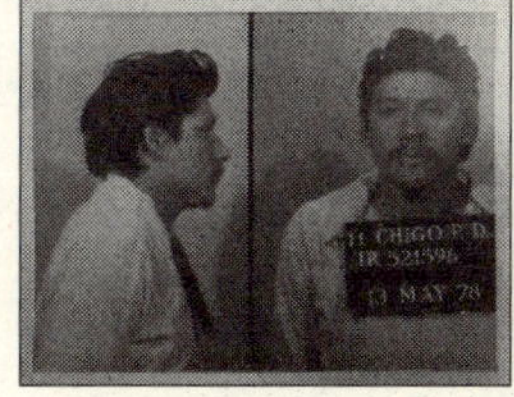
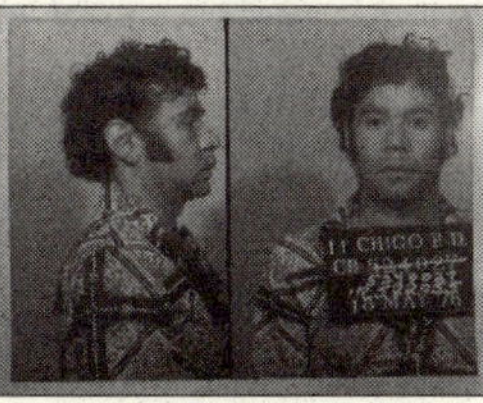

Figures 44–45. Jose Garcia Huerte and Cresenciano Sanchez *(courtesy of Chicago Police Department)*

- James Wheeler was part of a group of gang members who surrounded the victim, Willie Nix. Angered at Nix for refusing to join their gang, the group opened fire on the victim, shooting him some sixteen times. Yet he lived. He was a big man at the time of the shooting but was much thinner by trial. It was particularly dramatic when we asked him to remove his shirt and show the jury his wounds. His upper torso was covered with light dots against his dark skin from the scars. Guilty of attempted murder.

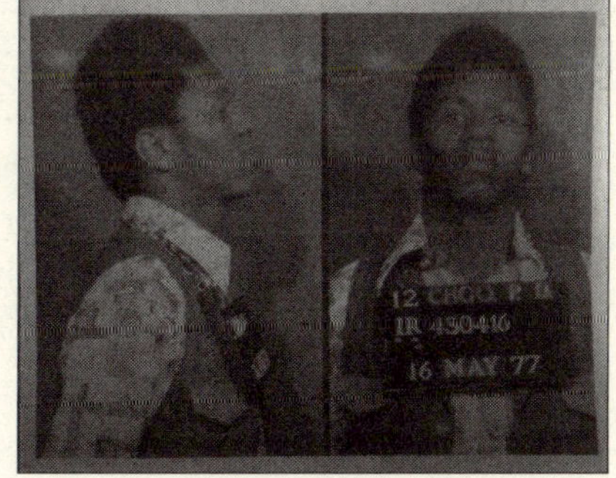

Figure 46. James Wheeler *(courtesy of Chicago Police Department)*

- Henry Lee Thomas awoke in the middle of the night, reached for a knife, and stabbed to death his girlfriend, Dorothy Terrell, who was asleep in bed next to him. After keeping her nude body in his apartment for three days, Thomas then rolled it into a quilt, carried it to his car, and dumped it in a forest preserve. We had to try the case after Judge Crowley suppressed the bloody physical evidence that was found in the defendant's car and apartment as the product of an illegal arrest without probable cause. But he ruled Thomas's court-reported confession was sufficiently attenuated from the arrest to make it admissible. Good thing, too. Without the physical evidence, the confession became the only evidence of his guilt.

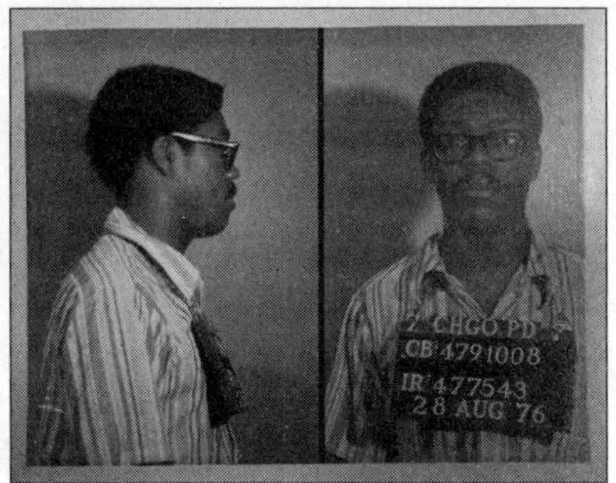

Figure 47. Henry Lee Thomas *(courtesy of Chicago Police Department)*

In the statement, Thomas told the assistant state's attorney, "I stabbed her in the neck and Dorothy waked up and said, 'What's wrong?'" He then said he stabbed her "two times, three times. Then I hit her in her face" before putting a pillow over her face to stifle her screams. During his opening statement, his attorney claimed that Henry was provoked by his pushy, abusive, flirtatious girlfriend. "Henry Thomas is not a brutal man," he told the jury. "Henry was the victim." He urged the jury to find him guilty of voluntary manslaughter. Nope. Guilty of murder—though on appeal, the court of appeals ruled that Judge Crowley erred in not suppressing the confession:

> The prosecution did not meet its burden of establishing that intervening events broke the causal connection between the illegal arrest and defendant's incriminating statements and therefore defendant's

> statements should have been suppressed. For that reason, his conviction must be reversed and the cause remanded for a new trial.

Without that statement and the already suppressed physical evidence, a new trial was impossible. Henry Lee Thomas had to be released from prison after serving just a little less than three years for the murder of Dorothy Terrell.

- Louis Chick committed a series of armed robberies of women at a 47th Street CTA train station on the South Side. After a jury trial with my partner Paul Tsukuno in front of Judge Grazian, Chick was found guilty. The next month, he pled guilty to another similar robbery. Judge Grazian sentenced him to the maximum of thirty years imprisonment and added an extra three years because Chick was on parole from a 1978 rape conviction.

Figure 48. Louis Chick
(courtesy of Chicago Police Department)

"Well, George, They're Letting Us Have Our Defense. They Must Not Think It Hurts Them Very Much"

MY TRIAL LAWYER days as an assistant state's attorney ended on a positive note. I returned to Judge Crowley's courtroom to 1st-chair the second of two murder trials against two brothers.

The brothers King—Robert and George—were from the West Side of Chicago. Robert had been a cellmate of a man named Gregory Perkins in the Stateville Penitentiary at Joliet, probably the most infamous prison in Illinois. After his release, Perkins began dealing drugs on the South Side of Chicago, while somehow maintaining his connection with Robert. Knowing Gregory was dealing drugs from his apartment, Robert figured he would have ample cash lying around. So Robert and George drove from the West Side to steal his drugs and money.

One argument for drug legalization is that those who deal in drugs must keep both cash and valuable product on their persons or in their domiciles and are extremely vulnerable to violent crime. In a sense, both Lonnie Butts and Gregory Perkins died not because of drugs, but because of drug laws.

When Gregory resisted the robbery, he was stabbed to death with a pair of scissors found at the bloody crime scene. (Notice the passive tense.)

Cops solve most cases on the basis of the victim or witnesses who know the perpetrator. If criminals committed crimes outside their immediate neighborhood (and wore masks), very few would get caught. But they rarely do.

The King brothers had indeed gone outside their neighborhood. And though they didn't wear masks, no one in this neighborhood knew them, so no one recognized them, and no one could tell the cops that "Joe did it." The homicide detectives were stumped at what appeared to be a stranger home invasion and murder.

In the real world, as opposed to the TV world, most homicide detectives just process the case based on a set of predetermined assumptions that have some basis in truth. For instance, that the spouse or boyfriend can reasonably be suspected. Only a small subset of homicide detectives are actual detectives like Hercule Poirot, or the kind we see on *Bosch*,

Law & Order, or pretty much every other police procedural. (For my money, *Bosch* was the best at depicting, within the constraints of a drama series, how real homicide detectives work to solve real cases.)

Homicide Investigator John Markham was one of those real detectives. Working out of Area 1 on the near South Side (the building from which that arrestee had escaped when I was on Felony Review and was left guarding two arrestees), Markham was assigned the case. He went to the crime scene and studied it.

At some point, he was flipping through Gregory Perkins's address book, which he'd found in the apartment. With a keen eye, he noticed something that struck him as possibly important: a name and number had been lined out yet were still visible. The name was Robert King.

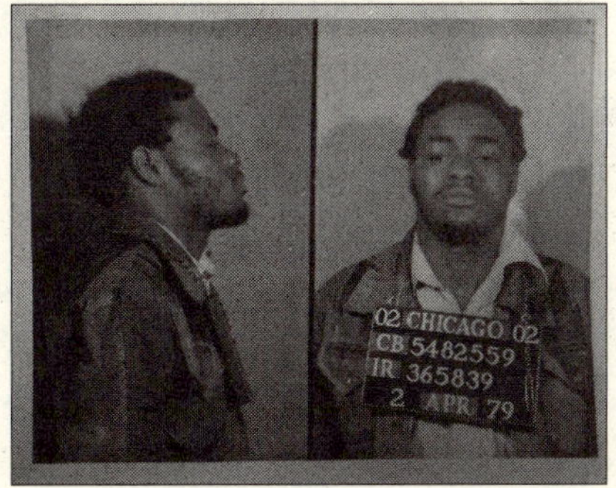

Figure 49. Robert King
(courtesy of Chicago Police Department)

Being an astute detective, Markham ran Robert King's rap sheet—as he had run Perkins's rap sheet—and found a long list of both charges and convictions, one of which had gotten him sent to Joliet, where (guess what) the two men had shared a cell. Bingo. Maybe this was no stranger murder after all.

Markham called the phone number in the address book next to Robert King's name. Robert King answered. Markham asked him a few questions. The way Robert King answered further raised Markham's suspicions. Soon after, both Robert and George were taken into custody and questioned about the murder of Gregory Perkins.

Sometime between the second and third days in custody, both brothers confessed to being there. In a show of brotherly love, each pointed the finger at the other as the stabber. After taking Robert's confession, Markham obtained a search warrant to search his apartment, where Gregory Perkins's keys and the proceeds of the robbery were found.

There's a third rule that, if criminals followed it, would cause cops' clearance rates to fall even lower: Don't talk to the police. Period. Just don't. As noted earlier, most "confessions" to the police are actually suspects trying to talk their way out of trouble, while actually talking themselves into prison.

Not all criminals are dumb. But it is the dumb ones who get caught and convicted. And Robert was particularly dumb. Instead of crossing out his own name, he could've just taken the address book and thrown it away. If he had, the murder of Gregory Perkins would be unsolved to this day.

While we would have liked to be able to prove which brother did the stabbing, we did not have the evidence to do so. But it didn't matter. Both were charged with felony murder. So legally it didn't matter who actually plunged the scissors into Perkins. All we had to prove to the jury was that both men were present at the robbery that ended with Perkins's death at the hands of one of them. But that's *if* we got to trial.

The brothers' defense attorneys each filed motions to suppress their confessions on the grounds that they'd been coerced by having been kept in custody for so long with insufficient reason to suspect that they'd committed the crimes. Had the confessions been suppressed, so too would have been the evidence found during the search of Robert's apartment that resulted from it.

Personally, I had no doubt that many cops in Chicago had coerced many confessions over the years. Some, perhaps most, confessors were indeed guilty, but at least some were innocent. In this case, given their association in prison and the crossed-out name in the address book, the police had an excellent reason to detain the brothers as they tried building a case against them, and had acted reasonably when doing so.

Judge Crowley denied the motion, but that didn't mean their attorneys wouldn't argue in court that the confessions, which would be read to the jury, had been coerced. Given how long they had been in custody before confessing, they might even be able to make a persuasive case. It was my job to ponder how I might reassure the jury that the police had acted reasonably.

That they were Joliet cellmates was a good basis for that. In the course of reviewing their prison disciplinary records, I also came across a report that they'd been caught *in flagrante delicto* by prison guards. Proving this, however, would not be easy. I would have had to identify the guards who witnessed them, subpoena them to come to Chicago from

Joliet, and hope they would make decent witnesses. We would then confront the defendant's objections to this evidence.

Most likely, the defense would object both to evidence of Robert's prior conviction and imprisonment and to proof of the sexual connection. And the defense would very likely succeed in claiming that the prejudicial impact of this information vastly outweighed any probative value in establishing the defendant's guilt. Remember, the only reason I wanted to offer all this testimony was to explain to the jury why the police acted reasonably in detaining the defendants for as long as they did. And the police didn't then know anything about the sexual connection between them. Concluding that none of this would be admissible if I tried to introduce it, I abandoned this strategy.

But that prep paid off.

Because the brothers each implicated the other in their confessions, their cases had to be severed so they could be tried separately. I could use George's out-of-court confession against him in his trial because it is considered an admission by him, which he could then deny on the witness stand, But I could not use George's confession accusing Robert of stabbing Gregory against Robert, because it was hearsay.

Hearsay is defined as an out-of-court statement offered to prove the truth of what the statement said. Moreover, Robert would be unable to cross-examine George about his accusation, which would violate his constitutional right to confront the witnesses against him. For these reasons, Robert and George each needed to be tried separately so I could use Robert's confession only against Robert, and George's confession only against George, but not use either of their confessions against the other.

My trial partner for the case against Robert King in Judge Crowley's court was Denny Dernbach, a good-natured, old-school prosecutor. Robert was represented by a public defender. In the end, the jury convicted Robert of 1st-degree murder.

Three months later, on August 31, 1981, after I was assigned to Judge Grazian and about a month before departing for the University of Chicago, I returned to Judge Crowley's court for my last jury trial as an assistant state's attorney by 1st-chairing the case against George King. My 2nd chair was Art Neville, who was just one year younger than me.

George's lawyer was James Kavanaugh, the former head of the Felony

Trial Division of the State's Attorney's Office, and my former boss. Jim had only recently gone into private practice, and, with the Public Defender's Office representing Robert, Judge Crowley appointed him to represent George.

During his opening statement, Kavanaugh told the jury his theory of the case. "No one contests the death of Gregory Perkins," he said. But "Robert King is the person who committed the crime."

"Robert's name was in Gregory's phone book."

"Gregory's keys were found in Robert King's bedroom."

Gregory's "property was in possession of Robert King."

Kavanaugh then contended that the murder of Gregory Perkins was completely disconnected from the robbery. It was instead a crime of passion arising out of the relationship between Robert and Gregory.

"Robert," he said, "was the homosexual lover of Gregory."

Kavanaugh's client George had nothing to do with this, he contended. Contributing to this theory was the fact that Gregory was stabbed to death using scissors that were in the apartment, suggesting that the crime was spontaneous and unplanned. He concluded: "The case will leave you full of doubt."

True, because the charge was felony murder, we did not have to prove any particular culpability of George's so long as we proved that he was a willing participant in the armed robbery, which resulted in Gregory's death. But all the defense needed was a peg to hang its hat on if they thought either that the brothers had been mistreated while in custody, or that George could not fairly be blamed for the alleged homicidal rage of his brother. So, given the evidence arrayed against George, Kavanaugh's play was smart. What else could he do?

As I had during the trial of Robert King, I put Detective Markham on the stand to describe the whole of the investigation. Then Kavanaugh got up to cross-examine.

"Detective Markham," he said, "in the course of your investigation, did you have occasion to learn—"

Let me hit pause here to note that whatever was going to complete this question would be calling for a hearsay answer. Before he finished the question, I knew it was objectionable on the grounds that the answer to the question would be something that someone had told Markham, not something that Markham had himself witnessed. And it was being offered by Kavanaugh to prove the truth of whatever out-of-court statement Markham had heard. As an experienced trial lawyer and trial judge, John Crowley knew this as well as I.

But before objecting, I waited to hear the rest of the question.

"—that Robert King, the defendant's brother, and Gregory Perkins were cellmates in the Illinois state penitentiary at Joliet."

I just sat there and didn't object. I didn't even move. After Markham answered in the affirmative, Kavanaugh launched into a series of questions eliciting hearsay about the nature of their relationship, and about their being caught by prison guards in a homosexual act. (Of course, per the rules of discovery, we had turned over the prison records to the defense.)

Sitting next to me, my 2nd chair, Art, started squirming uncomfortably in his seat. Why was the 1st chair allowing all this to come in? Why wasn't he objecting? Should he object instead, given that his 1st chair had apparently lost his mind? In the meantime, Judge Crowley was glaring at me from the bench. Had he used a gavel, he would have been holding it up and ready to strike. He'd once explained to me why he used a quarter coin rather than a gavel to rap on the bench: "If I had a gavel, I'm just going to end up throwing it at some lawyer."

At that moment, that lawyer would've been me.

Other judges under similar circumstances would've asked, "Counsel, do you have an objection to make?" In fact, Crowley himself would've asked that of many other lawyers. But by now, after all we had been through together over the past four years, he had enough confidence in me to know that just maybe I knew what I was doing.

Kavanaugh, of course, recognized immediately what was happening. After the next recess, when we returned to the courtroom, he told me what he told his client at the break: "Well, George, they're letting us have our defense. They must not think it hurts them very much."

Everything he'd gotten on the record was the information I'd wanted to introduce when prepping for trial. Now I didn't have to locate and bring in to court the prison guards. He was proving by hearsay what the court would have stopped me from proving by direct evidence. Now there'd be no question that the cops had acted properly, because they had an excellent reason to hold Robert.

Figure 50. View of the courtroom from Judge Crowley's bench

My entire thought process lasted less than a second. That's how long it had taken me to conduct a cost-benefit analysis and game out how this was going to go. From the time Kavanaugh finished his question to the time when Markham would answer it: a solitary, beautiful second.

When I think of all my jury trials as a prosecutor, the single moment of which I'm most proud is that non-objection. How funny. My finest moment as a prosecutor was keeping my mouth shut.

The verdict came in: guilty. Just like his brother.

George King was memorable for another reason. Normally, defendants did not react personally to my prosecuting them. Partly this was due to the fact that I never tried to demonstrate my "command" of the courtroom by, for example, sticking my finger in the defendant's face during closing arguments, as some prosecutors liked to do. I never made it personal. Indeed, after one jury trial, a defendant told me, "I wish you had been my lawyer."

George King was the first and only defendant who attempted to intimidate or dominate me by staring me down in the courtroom as he sat at the defense counsel table and I sat at the prosecution table. I am not a tough guy, and George King was a large, intimidating man. On the street, he would have made mincemeat out of me at five feet eleven, 160 pounds. But I simply could not permit him to get over on me—even if he and I were the only ones who would be aware of it.

So my Cal City upbringing kicked in, and I stared back at him until he looked away.

Thus ended my days fighting crime and corruption in Cook County, the most memorable years of my life. Little could I have known that the story was not yet over. Far from it.

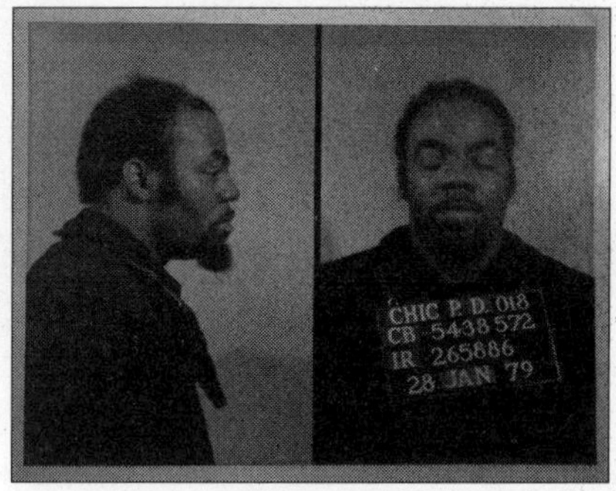

Figure 51. George King
(courtesy of Chicago Police Department)

Leaving the State's Attorney's Office

IN MY TWO years as a felony trial assistant, I had fourteen felony jury trials involving seventeen defendants. Half were for murder, four for rape. All but one was a *G*, or guilty verdict. The sole exception was the hung jury in my first jury trial, the one involving the caught-inside-residential burglar, Raymond Harding. I count the voluntary manslaughter verdict against Keith "Popeye" Hoddenbach as a *G* even though it might well have been a murder conviction had I done the proper legal research. (I also lost one of my two misdemeanor jury trials in Branch 46, but misdemeanors don't count. Right?)

While I am proud of my near-perfect record, it really is supposed to be this way. In Cook County, if the Felony Review assistants do their job and only approve charges where the evidence is sufficient for conviction, and the trial assistants do their job in presenting that evidence to the jury, the prosecutors are supposed to win. And they usually do.

But sometimes the prosecutors don't do their job the way they are supposed to. Just ask O. J. The prosecutorial failure in the O. J. Simpson case shows what happens when prosecutors who may be perfectly competent to handle the run-of-the-mill murder cases are elevated into the spotlight and cannot take the heat. When I was a felony trial assistant, William "Bill" Kunkle was the chief of the Criminal Prosecutions Bureau and Mike Ficaro headed the Felony Trial Division. Had O. J. committed his murder in Cook County when I was there, he would likely have been prosecuted by Kunkle, who prosecuted the mass murderer John Wayne Gacy, and Ficaro, who tried I-57 murderer Henry Brisbon. I believed thirty years ago, and believe today, that if Kunkle and Ficaro had tried the Simpson case instead of Marcia Clark and Christopher Darden, even O. J.'s "dream team" of defense lawyers would not have secured an acquittal.

In March of 1980, while I was a felony trial assistant, I took the opportunity to witness Bill Kunkle's dramatic closing argument in the Gacy case. John Wayne Gacy had murdered at least thirty-three young men and boys and buried many of their bodies in a crawl space beneath his suburban Chicago home. In excavating that space to remove their remains, the home was effectively demolished. But the trap door to the crawl space was preserved and brought into the courtroom, where it sat on a stand in front of a bulletin board with the eight-by-ten pictures of each of the victims.

Gacy had pled insanity (of course). The *New York Post* reported that "Defense psychiatrists linked Gacy's mental illness to his abusive father and said he projected hateful feelings onto his male sex partners and then was compelled to kill them." Kunkle addressed the defense's plea for mercy during his closing argument of the death penalty phase of the trial. In response, Kunkle told the jury they should show Gacy the same mercy he had shown his victims. He then removed the photos of each victim from the bulletin board and one by one, after reading their names, dropped each picture into the crawl space door where they hit the floor and scattered across the tile.

I was in the courtroom to witness that moment. I still have a copy of the *Chicago Sun-Times* with the headline: "Gacy found guilty." It is autographed by the prosecutors in the case. Bob Eagan wrote, "Jack did it." Terry Sullivan wrote, "The rat laughs no more." Bill Kunkle wrote, with his characteristically dark sense of humor: "John's favorite song: 'Mad about the Boy.'"

By a weird coincidence, on that same front page appeared a story about the arrest of Circuit Court Judge John J. ("J J") McDonnell (whom I mentioned in the chapter about misdemeanor jury trial auto theft court): "Controversial judge seized as drunken driver." The lede was: "Circuit Court Judge John J. McDonnell, suspended for four months in 1973 for waving a gun at a suburban couple, was arrested on drunken-driving charges early Wednesday."

The story featured this colorful detail, which reads like an episode of *Cops*: After being persuaded by the arresting state trooper to sit in the rear of his squad car, "the judge jumped out of the squad car and ran to his own auto and attempted to get the key into the ignition.... However, the judge was unable to insert the key, apparently because he had been drinking...." The paper noted that "McDonnell, who sits in [misdemeanor] Jury Court at 320 N. La Salle, was back on the bench hearing cases later Wednesday morning...." Otherwise he might have missed out on some bribes. This would not be the last newspaper story written about J J McDonnell.

Food: Energy-saving tips for the kitchen

Final markets
Race results

Sun-Times

Chicago, Thursday, March 13, 1980

Thursday
Red Streak

[illegible]; 25c elsewhere

Gacy found guilty

By Paul Galloway and Donald M. Schwartz

John W. Gacy was found guilty of 33 murders Wednesday by a jury that deliberated for only an hour and 50 minutes after a five-week trial.

Criminal Court Judge Louis B. Garippo immediately instructed the seven men and five women of the jury to return to the courtroom at 1:30 p.m. Thursday for what is expected to be a death penalty hearing in the mass-murder case.

The packed courtroom in the Criminal Courts Building at 26th and California heard the verdict in absolute silence after Garippo cautioned the audience against any reaction.

Garippo observed just before the verdict was announced that the jury might have to return for further deliberation [on a death penalty] and warned the audience against influencing the jury by any outcry.

Gacy also was found guilty of taking indecent liberties with a child and deviate sexual assault in the Robert Piest indictment.

The jury, in finding Gacy guilty of 33 murders of young men and boys—some of them involving sexual encounters—rejected the defense's lengthy presentation during the trial that Gacy was insane at the time of the killings.

Garippo also indicated after the verdict that he would continue to sequester the jury, which has been sequestered ever since it was selected in Rockford to hear the case here.

He also told the jurors not to "answer any inquiries now" about this case.

As Gacy left the courtroom, he smiled, winked and waved at a male court bailiff.

It took 10 minutes for the verdict to be read and the jury to

Turn to Page 18

Controversial judge seized as drunken driver

By Philip J. O'Connor

Circuit Court Judge John J. McDonnell, suspended for four months in 1973 for waving a gun at a suburban couple, was arrested on drunken-driving charges early Wednesday.

McDonnell, 45, was halted on the Illinois Tollway west of Highland Park at about 1:05 a.m. by state Trooper Richard Thomas, who said McDonnell's 1977 Oldsmobile was traveling unusually slow.

After his arrest, McDonnell first refused to get out of his auto and later leaped out of a squad car and tried to start his own auto, officers said. Then, after posting bond, he attempted to retrieve his auto from a towing firm against police advice, they said.

JUDGE JOHN J. McDONNELL

Thomas said he noticed McDonnell's northbound auto on the Tri-State Tollway (Interstate 94) north of Half Day Rd. (Illinois 22) and clocked it at 38 m.p.h., 7 m.p.h. less than the minimum required speed.

The trooper said he ordered McDonnell to stop and asked him to get out of his car, and that the judge refused.

Thomas said he then persuaded the judge to sit in the rear seat of his squad car while he made a radio check on McDonnell's auto license to make sure the auto was not stolen.

A short time later, the judge jumped out of the squad car

Turn to Page 74

Terrorists attack again in Puerto Rico

Puerto Rican police and FBI agents examine the shattered rear window of one of two cars that were hit by terrorist bullets Wednesday. This car happened to be hit as terrorists fired at a U.S. Army vehicle in San Juan. The military vehicle's three occupants, Army officers who teach [illegible] at the University of Puerto Rico, escaped with minor [illegible] flying glass. No other injuries were reported. It was the [illegible] terrorist attack on the U.S. military in Puerto Rico in [illegible] months. (UPI)

Stocks off 6.91, traders hesitant about inflation
Comment that inflation will be with us through 1980s helps give stocks a downward push. Page 76

Swift retiring at Sears; Brennan new president
A. Dean Swift leaving world's largest retailer for 'personal reasons.' Brennan to be successor. Page 76

Anderson may not back Reagan if he wins nod
Aide says it would be too hard to support a candidate 'whose views are so inimical' to Anderson's. Page 5

Collins beats Phillips 71-66 in triple overtime
High school takes a semi-final game in the Public League basketball playoffs at the Amphitheatre. Back Page

Figure 52. Autographed front page of *Chicago Sun-Times*
(courtesy of Chicago Sun-Times)

The Decline of the Cook County State's Attorney's Office

HAVING FAILED TO get a teaching job for the 1980–81 school year, I continued to serve as an assistant state's attorney. But during what turned out to be my last year in the office, with the help of my libertarian friends Walter Grinder and Leonard Liggio at the Institute for Humane Studies, I was able to raise the funds to pay for a year's salary as a research fellow. Thanks to the sponsorship of Professor Richard Epstein, whom I had come to know as a law student, I was able to spend the 1981–82 school year at the University of Chicago Law School, where I began developing my "consent theory of contract." As I mentioned earlier, with the gracious consent of Richard Devine, Richard Daley's 1st Assistant, I was given a year's leave of absence from the State's Attorney's Office, so I did not have to formally resign my position.

When I reentered the job market in the fall of 1981, nothing had changed about me except my affiliation. I was no longer a county prosecutor; I now held a researcher position at the University of Chicago. That difference in status, and that difference alone, resulted in my getting more than twenty-five interviews.

The day I finally resigned after landing a teaching job at Illinois Institute of Technology's Chicago-Kent College of Law, I made an appointment to see Rich Daley at his office in the Daley Center in the Chicago Loop. The building was named, of course, for his dad. I was just there to shake his hand and thank him for the job he had done and for treating me well. I found him to be an unassuming, almost humble guy—a far cry from the spoiled "Richie" Daley who had bullied his fellow Democrats in Springfield while his dad was alive. He went on to be a pretty decent mayor. Chicago could use him now.

Cook County could also use a decent State's Attorney. In 2020, Pat O'Brien, with whom I tried two jury trials in front of Judge Tom Maloney, ran as the Republican candidate against the Democrat Kim Foxx. In his campaign statement, O'Brien said,

> We must bring justice and integrity to Cook County. I pledge that the State's Attorney's Office will be

> professional, apolitical, and committed to the safety of the people of Cook County. In each of these areas, Kim Foxx has failed us.... I'm not a politician—I'm a former Cook County Judge, Cook County Assistant State's Attorney, Assistant Illinois Attorney General, and criminal defense attorney. I have spent my life securing justice for all. I've stood up to powerful politicians in both political parties, even when it meant sacrificing my career. Unlike many previous state's attorneys, especially Kim Foxx, I'm not looking for this position as a stepping-stone for higher office. My only agenda is to pursue justice for our hurting communities.

He lost. Foxx won. As a result, the downward spiral of crime in Chicago continued unabated. During Foxx's next term, several of her supervisors quit in disgust. James Murphy—a twenty-five-year veteran in the office—issued a public rebuke of the State's Attorney: "I would love to continue to fight for the victims of crime and to continue to stand with each of you, especially in the face of the overwhelming crime that is crippling our communities. However, I can no longer work for this Administration. I have zero confidence in their leadership. This Administration is more concerned with political narratives and agendas than with victims and prosecuting violent crime. That is why I can't stay any longer."

In 2024, Foxx announced she would be stepping down as Cook County State's Attorney. Eileen O'Neill Burke won the Democratic primary and then defeated the Republican candidate in the general election. Burke served as an assistant state's attorney, a defense attorney, and both a trial judge and appellate court judge. In her victory statement, she said: "We can build the best prosecutor's office in the country, where we set a new standard for integrity, effectiveness and innovation. Whether you voted for me or not, I promise you this: I will work tirelessly as your state's attorney."

The *Chicago Tribune* described Burke's background as a "Chicago native whose father, grandfather and great-grandfather worked for the Chicago Police Department." They omitted the fact that her husband,

John Burke, is the son of Alderman Edward M. Burke, who was the longstanding alderman for the 14th Ward until 2023, when he was found guilty of racketeering and bribery, leading to his conviction and sentencing in 2024.

This is not to taint the daughter-in-law for the sins of the father-in-law. After all, Rich Daley, the son of "Boss" Daley, was a good State's Attorney when I was there. Better a machine Democrat than a Soros-backed prosecutor any day of the week. It is only to observe that Chicago Democratic politics carries on.

Much to my surprise, so too did my own story of fighting crime and corruption in Chicago. Nearly two years after I left the State's Attorney's Office to be a law professor, something happened that colored my whole experience as a prosecutor in Cook County.

As they say on social media: "You won't believe what happened next."

PART IV: WHAT GOES AROUND WENT AROUND

A Surprise Happy Ending

IN THE FALL of 1982, I started teaching contract law at the Chicago-Kent College of Law. One day in August 1983, as I was about to commence my second year as a law professor, big news broke about a federal sting operation devised to uncover corruption in the Circuit Court of Cook County. In breaking the story, reporter Peter Karl called it "the largest undercover operation in the history of the Justice Department." That sounded like good news, but no details emerged. The story then went dormant, and I gave it little, if any, thought. News like this comes and goes in Chicago.

A few months later, while sitting in my office at Chicago-Kent, I got a call from Irv Miller, my old friend and partner in Judge Pincham's court, who was now a supervisor at 26th Street. Irv informed me that there was another leak. Reportedly, there had been an undercover mole who'd been working for the feds in the sting.

"Hey, partner," as he always called me, "we're all over here trying to figure out who the mole was. If it was you, you'd tell me, right?"

Apparently, I was a candidate because I'd gotten out after only four years to teach law, and also because I was Harvard Law, the thing that always made me a little different.

"Well, it wasn't me," I said.

"Well, how about Terry Hake?" he asked.

Terry. Yes. Terry. It was like an epiphany or moment of satori. Of course, it was Terry. It had to be, right? Terry's being the mole explained everything; the whole mystery of his behavior solved.

"Yes, that makes perfect sense," I said.

Some thirty minutes after I hung up the phone, I got another call, this one from Jane Fritsch. Jane was the criminal courts reporter for the *Chicago Sun-Times*, having come over to that paper from the *Chicago Tribune*, where I'd first met her when I was an ASA.

"I'm covering the story about the undercover mole," she told me.

"We've confirmed his identity is Terry Hake. And we were told you were a very good friend of his. So I'm calling you for any background you can give me because we're doing a front-page feature story about this. Anything you could give me, I'd appreciate."

"Sure," I said. "Very happy to talk to you 'bout Terry."

I went on for a while and referred to him as a Boy Scout. He was. I could've used "choir boy," the other term we commonly employ for people who are, well, Boy Scouts. Eventually, it would sink in that the proper word to describe Terry was "hero."

The next day, December 7, 1983—the anniversary of the Japanese sneak attack on Pearl Harbor, the "day that will live in infamy"—Fritsch's front-page story appeared with the big, bold headline "Key Greylord 'mole' named" and the kicker headline, "How 'Boy Scout' played shady lawyer role." My comments appeared on the front page right under the headline attributed to "a lawyer who was once a close friend of Hake." That was me. "In the last 24 hours I've had to go back and rewrite history," the quote began. "I was really kind of disappointed in Terry. I didn't understand why he was hanging out with such lightweight kinks. That's probably one reason why I didn't pursue our friendship. Now it seems quite obvious what was going on." I then added, "He was always such a Boy Scout. Then he started hanging out with slime. But he was a bigger Boy Scout than any of us ever knew." Another unnamed former colleague of his referred to him as "a legitimate hero for all the right reasons."

The next day, Terry and I reconnected on the phone. It was like a reunion. After more than four years of being estranged, we talked the way we used to for at least two hours. He told me a lot about the undercover sting, dubbed Operation Greylord; how he'd been asked to join; his willingness to endure whatever came his way, even though he knew it would change his life and cost him friends; and that he'd even been sworn in as an FBI agent for the duration of the investigation.

He told me he was relieved when I stopped calling him to socialize, because it was too difficult to have to misrepresent himself to his closest friends. Nor could he confide in me. The only two persons in whom he could confide were his mom and his then-fiancée, Cathy. He could not even tell his father out of concern that Dad might tell others.

FASHION: 264 gift ideas —inexpensive to out of sight

SPORTS: De Paul romps, Illini, Ind. win; Celts rip Bulls

SHOW: Mitzi Gaynor in spotlight at Arie Crown

COLD
A 30 percent chance of snow; high in the mid- or upper 20s. Page 50.

Sun-Times

5★ Sports Final

CHICAGO, WEDNESDAY, DECEMBER 7, 1983 25¢ CITY, SUBURBS 40¢ ELSEWHERE

INSIDE:
Bernardin calls for 'ethic of life' Page 4
$12 million paid for book Page 5
Spacelab voids Nobel theory Page 38
New U.S. Steel closing threat Page 73

Key Greylord 'mole' named

How 'Boy Scout' played shady lawyer role

By Jane Fritsch

He has the face of a choirboy, a ready smile and the key to the most ambitious investigation of judicial corruption in the nation's history.

His name is Terry Hake, a 32-year-old lawyer from a Chicago suburb, who spent the last three years posing as a shady attorney to expose corruption in the Cook County courts.

He played the role so well that some old friends and colleagues shunned him.

As word swept through the legal community Tuesday that he was a "mole" at the center of the U.S. Justice Department's Operation Greylord, some lawyers who knew him expressed astonishment that he had fooled so many people for so long.

"In the last 24 hours I've had to go back and rewrite history," said a lawyer who once was a close friend of Hake. "I was really kind of disappointed in Terry.

"I didn't understand why he was hanging around with such lightweight kinks. That's probably one reason why I didn't pursue our friendship. Now it seems quite obvious what was going on.

"He was always such a Boy Scout. Then he started hanging out with slime. But he was a bigger Boy Scout than any of us ever knew."

In his undercover role as an assistant state's attorney, Hake accepted bribes to

See GREYLORD, Page 4

PLO bus bomb kills 4 in Israel; reprisal vowed

By Norman Kempster
Los Angeles Times

JERUSALEM—A powerful bomb blew apart a crowded city bus Tuesday, killing four passengers and injuring 46, some of them critically. The Palestine Liberation Organization took responsibility for the terrorist attack, the bloodiest in Jerusalem in more than five years.

- Marine barrage silences Druze guns. Page 9.
- Situation brings call for Congress return. Page 9.
- Marines in Beirut could haunt Reagan. Page 9.

Prime Minister Yitzhak Shamir vowed that "the perpetrators of this wicked assault . . . will not remain unpunished," but military forces took no immediate reprisal action. Often in the past, Israeli planes have bombed Palestinian positions in Lebanon in response to terrorist attacks.

Tuesday's bombing was the first in Israel in more than four years that resulted in the loss of civilian lives, though hidden bombs are found and defused regularly throughout the country.

The attack came less than a month after a car bomb

See BOMB, Page 8

Paramedics pull bodies from the wreckage after a bomb blew apart a crowded bus in Jerusalem Tuesday, killing four people. The Palestine Liberation Organization took responsibility for the attack. (AP)

Figure 53. Front page story about Terry Hake and Operation Greylord
(courtesy of Chicago Sun-Times)

It is worth reflecting on the difference between Terry and me. My father had taught me to be very cynical about corruption in Cook County. So, bad as it was, I was pleasantly surprised that the State's Attorney's Office was not corrupt, too, as I had expected it to be. I was invigorated to resist the corruption I encountered in the misdemeanor branch courts. It never occurred to me to go outside the system or to quit. Fighting corruption within the system was one of the things that made being a real prosecutor better than TV.

In contrast, Terry entered the system with his ideals intact, and his confrontation with its corruption left him deeply depressed. As he later told me, "I called up [Mike] Ficaro and told him I just can't take it anymore."

"Don't quit the office," Ficaro replied.

Terry told him he wanted to go back to Felony Review. "There my depression went away immediately," he later told me.

When the feds contacted the leadership of the State's Attorney's Office looking for someone who might assist their investigation, Ficaro told them about Terry.

In May 1980, after an extensive vetting, Terry left Felony Review to be sworn in as an FBI special agent. He was then transferred to Branch 57 drug court to pose as a crooked prosecutor. (For the whole story, read Terry's 2015 book, *Operation Greylord: The True Story of an Untrained Undercover Agent and America's Biggest Corruption Bust*.)

In our reunion phone call, I remember asking Terry what the feds were doing for his protection. Not much, he said. They installed an alarm system in his home, but basically told him not to worry. I thought Terry was, once again, being naive. Dean "the Dream" Wolfson, one of the corrupt lawyers who was deeply implicated in Greylord, but who had not yet been charged with anything, had represented a ton of killers. All he had to do was ask one of them for a favor.

But Terry was still as idealistic as he had been when he entered the criminal justice system and was appalled by the corruption he saw. Only this time he was idealistic about the feds. He did not have a father like mine who raised him to be aware of what the Chicago political system under "Boss" Daley was all about. He had apparently not watched *Kojak*, in which the feds were depicted as intermeddlers in the real law enforcement efforts of the homicide detectives in Manhattan South.

After the exposure of the investigation, the federal indictments and arrests came in a flurry. Every corrupt judge before whom I had appeared was indicted and convicted, which is why I have been able to write about them being crooked with the certitude I did—and no fear of a defamation suit. "JJ" McDonnell, Jack Reynolds, and yes, John "Dollars" Devine, as well as many more. Likewise, Edward Kaplan, the kink lawyer who shared his bond-slip money with Devine. Kaplan pled guilty and was sentenced to two years in prison for bribing judges.

Figure 54. Judge John J. McDonnell leaves the federal building in 1988. His was the last major judicial case related to Operation Greylord. *(courtesy of Frank Hanes/Chicago Tribune)*

Figure 55. Former Judge John F. Reynolds leaves the Dirksen U.S. Courthouse in 1986 after being sentenced in a case related to Operation Greylord *(courtesy of Jerry Tomaselli/Chicago Tribune)*

But there was still one more big surprise to come: Judge Thomas Maloney got exposed in a separate federal sting operation called Operation Gambat.

"Rigging Murder Cases for Cash"

IN CONTRAST WITH the contempt I felt for these other corrupt judges, I had found Tom Maloney to be a knowledgeable trial judge who knew the rules of evidence, controlled his courtroom, was fair to both sides, and gave no hint of being the kind of judge who was on the take. Over the years, he'd impressed quite a number of people besides me.

"In his courtroom," wrote the *Chicago Tribune*, "Mr. Maloney presided under a framed portrait of legendary U.S. Supreme Court Chief Justice John Marshall and was known for imposing tough sentences and castigating gang members as 'the lowest sorts of cowards.' He was also tough on lawyers, demanding they be prepared before they stood before him. For a time, he was one of six so-called 'heater' judges who were assigned high-profile cases."

But Tom Maloney was one other thing as well: He was a former lawyer for the mob who fixed murder cases for money, both as a lawyer and as a judge.

The charges brought against him were, if anything, the most serious of any judge charged. "At a six-week trial that ended in April 1993," the *Chicago Tribune* reported, "Maloney, a judge for thirteen years, was convicted of" the following:

- Taking $10,000 to fix the double-murder trial of two El Rukn leaders in 1986, three years after the government's undercover Operation Greylord probe of court corruption became public. Maloney apparently suspected the FBI was onto the fix and personally handed the cash back to corrupt attorney William Swano near his chambers, testified Swano. ... Maloney convicted the two Rukns of the double murder, and a jury later sentenced them both to death.
- Sharing in an undetermined part of $100,000 in bribes for acquitting three New York gang members in 1981 for the murder of a rival in Chicago's Chinatown.
- Pocketing $4,000 to $5,000 to find accused murderer Owen Jones guilty of a reduced charge of voluntary manslaughter in 1982.

Moreover, during the sentencing procedure after his conviction, federal prosecutors charged that “although difficult to imagine, Thomas Maloney’s life of corruption was considerably more expansive than proved at trial.” The *Tribune* reported the prosecutors’ allegation that, as a judge, “Maloney fixed Spilotro’s 1983 trial for the murders of two small-time burglars, William McCarthy and James Miraglia, 21 years earlier. … Spilotro and his brother, Michael, were [later] killed in a celebrated mob hit in 1986.”

The primary witness to the fix of the Spilotro case was Robert Cooley. Cooley, who’d been “a longtime corrupt attorney … went undercover for the government beginning in 1986.” I knew Robert Cooley from my days in misdemeanor branch courts. He was the brother of Dennis Cooley, who was my supervisor in Branch 64—the one who’d counseled me on how to channel my anger against attorney Eddie Genson for fixing a case out from under me. Dennis’s brother Bob was a kink.

These revelations about Tom Maloney were enough to make me realize that no amount of cynicism about corruption in Cook County could ever encompass reality. My dad’s lessons about expecting corruption as a default position turned out to be true, just not true enough.

“The government also alleged that as a lawyer Maloney paid numerous cash bribes to former Judge Maurice Pompey in the 1970s by using convicted former bailiff Lucius Robinson as a bagman.” But Pompey was never prosecuted and eventually retired to Arizona. “In addition, the government alleged Maloney’s bagman attempted to fix the trial of Dino Titone for a drug-related double murder, but the effort fell through and the judge convicted Titone and sentenced him to death.”

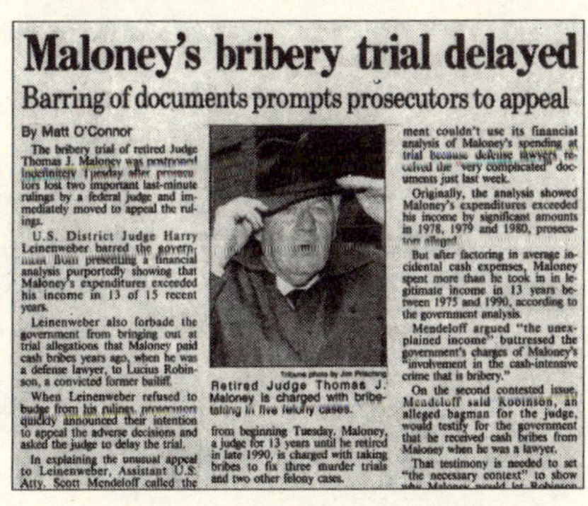

Maloney’s bribery trial delayed

Barring of documents prompts prosecutors to appeal

By Matt O’Connor

The bribery trial of retired Judge Thomas J. Maloney was postponed indefinitely Tuesday after prosecutors lost two important last-minute rulings by a federal judge and immediately moved to appeal the rulings.

U.S. District Judge Harry Leinenweber barred the government from presenting a financial analysis purportedly showing that Maloney’s expenditures exceeded his income in 13 of 15 recent years.

Leinenweber also forbade the government from bringing out at trial allegations that Maloney paid cash bribes years ago, when he was a defense lawyer, to Lucius Robinson, a convicted former bailiff.

When Leinenweber refused to budge from his rulings, prosecutors quickly announced their intention to appeal the adverse decisions and asked the judge to delay the trial.

In explaining the unusual appeal to Leinenweber, Assistant U.S. Atty. Scott Mendeloff called the

Retired Judge Thomas J. Maloney is charged with bribe-taking in five felony cases.

from beginning Tuesday. Maloney, a judge for 13 years until he retired in late 1990, is charged with taking bribes to fix three murder trials and two other felony cases.

ment couldn’t use its financial analysis of Maloney’s spending at trial because defense lawyers received the “very complicated” documents just last week.

Originally, the analysis showed Maloney’s expenditures exceeded his income by significant amounts in 1978, 1979 and 1980, prosecutors alleged.

But after factoring in average incidental cash expenses, Maloney spent more than he took in in legitimate income in 13 years between 1975 and 1990, according to the government analysis.

Mendeloff argued “the unexplained income” buttressed the government’s charges of Maloney’s “involvement in the cash-intensive crime that is bribery.”

On the second contested issue, Mendeloff said Robinson, an alleged bagman for the judge, would testify for the government that he received cash bribes from Maloney when he was a lawyer.

That testimony is needed to set “the necessary context” to show

Figure 56. Newspaper clipping of article about Judge Thomas J. Maloney *(courtesy of Chicago Tribune)*

Thomas J. Maloney was sentenced to sixteen years in federal prison, of which he served twelve. He died, at age eighty-three, in a nursing home within a year of his release. Ever the con man, he professed his innocence to the end.

* * *

In my four years as an assistant state's attorney, I had a pretty good sense of who was "straight" and who was "bent." But twice I was seriously fooled, once in each direction. I wrongly believed my good friend Terry Hake had become a corrupt lawyer instead of an undercover hero. And I wrongly believed Tom Maloney to be a good trial judge instead of someone who, as described in his *Chicago Tribune* obituary, was "the first—and remains the only—Cook County judge to be convicted of rigging murder cases for cash."

Breaking Down on the Witness Stand

WHEN JOHN DEVINE went on trial in federal court, guess who his defense attorney was? Good old Eddie Genson. Maybe if there'd been dispositive proof of his distributing payouts, Genson would have gone down, too. Instead, he received glowing profiles in the press and even taught as an adjunct professor at the Chicago-Kent College of Law, my first professorial home. In 1989, *The American Lawyer* magazine dubbed him a "trickster." With "old-time wiles and tireless preparation, Genson, 48, has confounded, irritated, and enraged prosecutors in Chicago for two decades. At the same time, he's established himself as one of the city's most sought after criminal defense lawyers."

Well, I was certainly one prosecutor whom he "enraged," but *not* due to his "tireless preparation."

The magazine also noted that "he befriended the lawyers and state judges he later represented at reduced fees during the code-named 'Greylord' investigation of corruption among Chicago judges, lawyers, and court officers. 'You don't abandon people who were there at the beginning,' Genson says. 'I've kept all my old friends.'"

More to the point, you also don't abandon the judges and lawyers whom you bribed and who could implicate you in their corruption. In fact, you even give those lawyers a discount. My guess is that he repped them all pro bono because the answer to cui bono was Eddie Genson himself.

One of the lawyers both befriended by and represented by Genson was Dean "the Dream" Wolfson—the lawyer who had sent a warning to me not to bad-mouth him. After Wolfson pled guilty to racketeering, Eddie Genson organized a campaign featuring letters from more than one hundred judges, prosecutors, defense attorneys, and other persons on his behalf. They praised him for his gentility, generosity, charity, and integrity. They might also have mentioned he was a dapper dresser. Wolfson was sentenced to seven and a half years in federal prison.

But Genson himself was never charged or even implicated. I know what I know about him from personal experience.

At Devine's trial in federal court, Genson cross-examined Terry for three days. He persisted in portraying Terry as fundamentally dishonest—which, of course, one has to be when one is an undercover agent—and unlikeable for turning his best friend in to the feds.

Here's a sample of Genson's approach.

"In your conversation [with Matt] you made no attempt to discourage your good friend, the one who talks to you about his wedding, and baby, from bribing, or attempting to bribe the judge, did you, sir?"

"No, I did not."

"And would that have influenced or hurt your role as a law enforcement officer of the FBI if you had told your friend, 'Look, just stop all this and start practicing law the right way'? You wouldn't have to uncover your identity by doing that, would you, sir?"

"No. But it would have been wrong for me to let it go by my eyes, too, Mr. Genson, as a law enforcement officer."

On the third day, I walked from my office at Chicago-Kent on Wacker Drive to the federal district court located in the Dirksen Federal Building in the Downtown Loop. I went to show moral support for my friend, but also get the moral satisfaction of seeing the guy who fixed that chop shop case out from under me answer for his corruption. Devine looked over at me as I sat near the aisle in the spectator's section. Did he recognize me after all these years?

During a recess, Devine walked up the aisle. As he passed where I was sitting, he said, "Hi, Randy."

Sheerly by reflex, I said, "Hi, Judge," and immediately wished I hadn't. He wasn't a judge anymore and didn't deserve the honorific, but I'd only ever called him "Judge," so that's what popped out.

After Genson had concluded his cross-examination, I left the court to use the restroom. When I returned, I found that the court was in recess because Terry had broken down on the witness stand, not during cross-examination, but during redirect by the assistant U.S. attorney. As his friend, I was ushered back to the witness room where he was sitting, being consoled, and trying to compose himself. I joined in with the consoling.

In his book, *Operation Greylord*, Terry remembered it this way:

> A law professor friend of mine, Randy Barnett, came in wanting to know what happened to me on the

> stand. Barnett was attending the trial as a spectator but had gone to the bathroom while I was still testifying, and when he returned the trial was in recess and a former public defender was complimenting Genson for his attack on me. I couldn't explain without crying again, not with someone else near us, so I took Barnett to the empty hallway and told him what I could. But some things you can't explain. All the education you go through from kindergarten through law school doesn't prepare you for the human heart.

So what had happened that shook up Terry so badly?

Genson's defense strategy had been to go after Terry's character, hoping to paint him in the jury's mind as deceitful, dishonest, and not to be believed. To prove the point, he pressed him on how he had turned in his close friend Matt to the feds. If you've seen the film about the Abscam scandal, *American Hustle*, think of the scene near the end when the grifter who'd gotten busted (played by Christian Bale), and henceforth had to work undercover for the FBI, revealed to the mayor of Camden (Jeremy Renner), whom he'd grown to love, that the feds would soon be there for him. It was excruciating, the mix of sadness, regret, and betrayal.

The difference here, with Terry, was that he wasn't doing this to save himself from prison. He was doing it to clean up the corruption in this notoriously corrupt city he loved. Terry realized that if he gave Matt a pass on this conversation, he would be doing exactly what he was trying to combat.

With no one besides his mother and his fiancée in whom to confide, before turning in Matt, Terry had gone to visit his mom to tell her what he was about to do. As he told her, he'd broken down. When the assistant U.S. attorney asked Terry on redirect about the personal toll his work had taken on him, Terry told the jury, "I went home and cried to my mother."

In his book, Terry explains why. "Not only had I discovered that I had lost my closest friend at the State's Attorney's Office to corruption, I had been forced out of the illusion of basic human goodness that had sheltered me all my life." Remembering and describing that emotional moment with his mom brought back all those feelings, causing Terry to break down in front of the jury.

"Do you want a recess?" asked the judge. Terry was unable to answer because he was weeping so hard. "I found myself crying, and couldn't collect my feelings once the first words tumbled out. I held my hands up in a time-out signal."

"Let's take five minutes," the judge said.

"I had steeled myself for the cross-examination," he wrote, "but let myself be open during the redirect. That was when the deepness of my emotions caught me by surprise." Relating the memory of his confession to his mother had dredged up all the same feelings, and he was overcome once again.

Thankfully, the jury did not buy Genson's shabby defense theory. But his characterization of Terry as a "rat" was shared by a surprising number of otherwise respectable lawyers in the criminal justice system—including some lawyers I'd always admired. After I heard what they thought of Terry, I never again looked at them the same way.

Matt would turn state's evidence in return for immunity, testifying against the several judges he had paid off. But he rightfully lost his law license. His brother told a *Tribune* reporter, "To the average person, that's diddly, but for our family, it was big. The whole process was horrible."

In a way, however, Greylord had saved Matt's life. I saw what happened to the fixers as they grew old. Many were pathetic scum. All were morally hollow. Greylord gave Matt a second chance, and, from what I can tell by looking online, he used it to live a successful life. On the off chance that someone reading this book might know him, I have chosen not to use Matt's real name. Terry made the same choice in his book.

For two years, Terry was the lead trial witness against most every major defendant nabbed by Operation Greylord. Every defendant was convicted. So obviously the FBI rewarded him for his brave, noble, selfless service. Right?

Well, if you know how to cough a cynical laugh, now's the time.

When it was all over, Terry told his superiors he wanted to stay in Chicago. They said, Oh no, Chicago's a plum assignment. *You have to go off to some small field office somewhere in the boonies and work your way back to Chicago some years down the line.*

How's that for gratitude?

Terry resigned from the FBI and became chief of security for the Chicago and North Western Railroad, then took a few other positions before finally returning to the Cook County State's Attorney's Office, prosecuting felonies. Once he reached retirement age, he left. His daughter is now an assistant state's attorney.

I suppose there's an irony in all this. One of the reasons that Terry was originally approached to go undercover was that he'd made no secret of his disgust with the corrupt system he'd confronted as an ASA. My response to all the dirt I saw in the system was quite different. I was my very cynical father's mostly cynical son.

I'd grown up hearing about crooked cops and assumed Chicago was *Chinatown*; everything was crooked. Indeed, as I've previously mentioned, I fully expected the State's Attorney's Office to be bent as well. The office under Bernie Carey had turned out to be remarkably clean. So too under Rich Daley. That subjective impression of mine was confirmed by the fact that no one in our office was implicated by Operation Greylord.

Over the course of my time there, only a couple of people out of 550 lawyers in our office ever left under a cloud, and I was generally unaware of even these. So, unlike Terry, who was deeply disillusioned, I was pleasantly surprised! Of course, when I was an ASA, no one like Edward Kaplan or Eddie Genson ever had to approach me or my fellow prosecutors to offer us bribes to fix a case. They didn't need us. They had the cops and the judges.

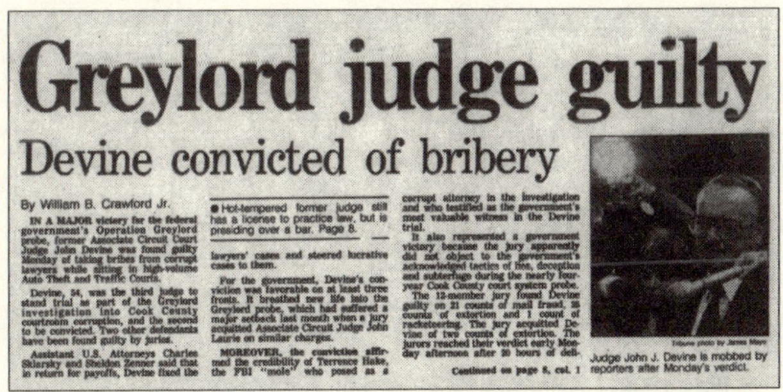

Greylord judge guilty

Devine convicted of bribery

By William B. Crawford Jr.

IN A MAJOR victory for the federal government's Operation Greylord probe, former Associate Circuit Court Judge John Devine was found guilty Monday of taking bribes from corrupt lawyers while sitting in high-volume Auto Theft and Traffic Courts.

Devine, 34, was the third judge to stand trial as part of the Greylord investigation into Cook County courtroom corruption, and the second to be convicted. Two other defendants have been found guilty by juries.

Assistant U.S. Attorneys Charles Sklarsky and Sheldon Zenner said that in return for payoffs, Devine fixed the lawyers' cases and steered lucrative cases to them.

● Hot-tempered former judge still has a license to practice law, but is presiding over a bar. Page 8.

For the government, Devine's conviction was favorable on at least three fronts. It breathed new life into the Greylord probe, which had suffered a major setback last month when a jury acquitted Associate Circuit Judge John Laurie on similar charges.

MOREOVER, the conviction affirmed the credibility of Terrence Hake, the FBI "mole" who posed as a corrupt attorney in the investigation and who testified as the government's most valuable witness in the Devine trial.

It also represented a government victory because the jury apparently did not object to the government's acknowledged tactics of lies, deception and subterfuge during the nearly four-year Cook County court system probe.

The 12-member jury found Devine guilty on 21 counts of mail fraud, [illegible] counts of extortion and 1 count of racketeering. The jury acquitted Devine of two counts of extortion. The jurors reached their verdict early Monday afternoon after 20 hours of deli-

Continued on page 8, col. 1

Judge John J. Devine is mobbed by reporters after Monday's verdict.

Figure 57. Newspaper clipping of article describing Judge John J. Devine's conviction *(courtesy of Chicago Tribune)*

So my story of fighting crime and corruption as an assistant state's attorney in Cook County had a happy ending worthy of TV. But what

I experienced along the way during my four years was better than anything I've ever seen on TV. That little kid who'd fallen in love with *The Defenders* had grown up to do work that surpassed even that father and son.

POSTSCRIPT: BETTER THAN TV?

The Problem with Hollywood Prosecutors

SOME YEARS AGO, a movie producer named Sky Conway recruited me to help with a script for a feature film called *InAlienable* and offered me a small role in the movie playing a prosecutor, an amazing

Figure 58. The author and Marina Sirtis in *InAlienable* *(courtesy of Sky Conway)*

experience I describe in *A Life for Liberty*. But that was not my first encounter with Hollywood. My first encounter was when I offered some famous producers my unsolicited opinion about the portrayal of prosecutors on television.

On January 15, 1981, *Hill Street Blues* premiered on NBC as a mid-season replacement series. Set in Chicago, and filmed partially on location, its gritty portrayal of beat cops and plain-clothes tactical officers was groundbreaking. Now in my fourth and final year as a Cook County State's Attorney, it captured my imagination. But it also triggered a criticism. Prosecutors were almost never depicted accurately in either cop shows or lawyer shows, and I'd always overlooked that. For this show though, I felt impelled to say something. This show, I thought, had the potential to do it right.

On February 5, my twenty-ninth birthday, I sent a lengthy letter to its showrunners, Steven Bochco and Michael Kozoll. I also mailed a copy to Grant Tinker, the head of MTM Productions—the company named after Tinker's wife, Mary Tyler Moore.

Mr. Steven Bochco
Mr. Michael Kozoll
MTM Productions
CBS Studio Center
4004 Radford
Studio City, CA 91604

Gentlemen:

Hill Street Blues is a unique and largely successful attempt to capture the spirit of big city police work within a one-hour television program. To criticize the show for any lack of realism is to compliment the effort since no one expects a "cop show" to be realistic and, despite the inherent limitations of an entertainment format, HSB obviously respects its subject. It is because of this I am writing to point out a dimension of everyday law enforcement which, though largely ignored thus far on HSB, where mentioned is distorted by too heavy a reliance on the type of cliches that HSB is seeking to avoid. The area I refer to is the legal profession and in particular, the prosecutor and defense attorney.

Since the tradition of TV lawyers is so well established, it would be natural for *HSB* to accept it at face value. But with a very few exceptions—*The Defenders, For The People* with William Shatner, *The Law* with Judd Hirsch (a made-for-TV movie and miniseries) and *Helter Skelter* come to mind—television has yet to display any understanding of how prosecutors, defense attorneys, and police officers really interact.

I have watched every lawyer show from *Perry Mason* to *Petrocelli* and every cop show from *Dragnet* to *Baretta* for as many episodes as it took to realize that a program rather than explore its subject, used that subject as a convenient plot device to present melodrama, missing in the process that which makes law enforcement fascinating.

This is not unique to the genre. Such break-through shows as *Lou Grant, White Shadow, East Side, West Side,* and *Slattery's People* with Richard Crenna in their respective genres are exceptions that prove the rule. These shows and a few others seek to draw dramatic situations from the subject at hand by attempting to portray what the subject is really all about. Comparing *Lou Grant* to *The Name of the Game* should adequately illustrate the point. The former is about the newspaper business while the latter is about what thrilling dangers faced Gene Barry (or Robert Stack, or Tony Franciosa). *HSB* is not the first such attempt in this genre of course. Susskind's *N.Y.P.D.* and, in its early days, *Kojak* preceded it. But in their grim seriousness, both shows missed a vital aspect of police work that *HSB*, like *M*A*S*H* and *Rockford*, relies on: humor (as opposed to comedy).

Until *Kojak* and *Rockford*, however, the existence of prosecutors and defense attorneys was unknown in the world of the TV cop. In fact, the dichotomy between TV lawyer and TV cop is so radical that you can select jurors by knowing which type of show they prefer—cop shows where the accused is always guilty or lawyer shows where defendant is always innocent. While *Kojak* and *Rockford* acknowledged the existence of the DA and defense attorney, both accepted the TV stereotype of the defense attorney, and because none previously existed they created a new one for the prosecutor.

The criminal defense lawyer was still either a bright, eager, liberal crusader defending the poor and innocent and frustrated by "the system," e.g. Gretchen Corbett's Beth Davenport on *Rockford*, or a slick, high priced, slightly unscrupulous defender of rich and guilty criminals exploiting "the system" (Jack Somack's brilliant portrayal of Isaac Hayes' defense attorney on *Rockford* is one exception). The prosecutor is now a well-meaning, somewhat bookish if not effete lawyer who, though knowledgeable about the law, is obviously naive about the plight of the poor cop. These usually harried attorneys are forever frustrated by what they perceive to be the bumbling of the cop who must deal with the reality of catching bad guys (always murderers) who play by no rules, and they typically display this frustration in the rudest, most boorish and arrogant manner. (Ironically, this portrayal of the TV DA is in my experience a more reasonable characterization of a young civil attorney from a "good" law school in a prestigious large law firm—perhaps the source of the image.) The prosecutor is portrayed as just one more obstacle in the path of good police work.

I am not so much criticizing the sometimes unforgivable legal inaccuracies, the all-time classic of which has to be the release of the crazed killer in "Dirty Harry" because Clint Eastwood had made a bad arrest and search—which he had—even though there was eye witness evidence of guilt and a serious charge of attempted murder of a police officer that still existed. Rather it is with both the characterization of the lawyer and the lawyers' actual relationship to the police that has yet to be suitably treated. *HSB* is no exception. Presumably to provide an off-beat love interest and an opposing view point, the principal lawyer character is a defense attorney who, with her friends' observing the traditional stereotype, is young, beautiful, well-bred, well educated, liberal, tough, supremely confident and, as always, "very good." Even the name "Davenport" is an unconscious copy. The DA to date has been invisible, though references to how the on-screen defense lawyers plan to deal with the faceless DA are absurd. When he or she does make an appearance, I predict that the new DA stereotype, possibly a bit mellowed out and more sympathetic, will be adhered to.

So what, then, is the true prosecutor like and what is

the relationship between the prosecutor and the police? I can only speak from my experience in Chicago and to a much lesser extent in Cambridge and Boston, but though I consider the Cook County State's Attorney's Office under Richard M. Daley to be exceptionally well run, I don't think it is unusual in most relevant respects.

First of all, the Assistant State's Attorneys who make it through the system to the felony trial courts are not typical lawyers and bear no relation to large law firm associates either in demeanor or sensibilities. Prestigious law firms are extensions of "good" law schools both in values and in that they inhabit the same legal and social worlds. Prosecutors are products of the criminal-justice system, and regardless of their legal education, whether Ivy or city law school (overwhelmingly the latter), they emerge as individuals with similar attitudes and sensibilities as the patrolmen and detectives they are in intimate contact with from their first day as attorneys. The difference in education and salary can create a very real social gap between prosecutor and policeman, but both are usually drawn from the same urban, ethnic background, and their common professional experience produces a collegiality that has unaccountably been missed in TV dramatizations (*Helter Skelter* is an illustrative exception). Where do so-called technical consultants come from? Do they understand the nature of their own work? Do the writers and producers pay attention to their advice? This has long puzzled me.

Prosecutors in my office do not only work closely with police in a courtroom environment. While assigned to our Felony Review Unit, an Assistant works exclusively with the police, does not go to court, and is officed right in the police station. His or her function is to counsel the police, review evidence, and evaluate and screen criminal charges. In Cook County, felony charges must be approved by Felony Review before the police may place them. Felony Review operates around the clock, seven days a week. The Felony Review Assistant often participates in ongoing investigations, reviewing all search and arrest warrants, advising on proposed police conduct, investigating any incident involving police shootings and, most importantly, interviewing witnesses and accused persons in the station, obtaining confessions where appropriate, and later testifying in court.

Relatively inexperienced Assistants in this assignment can have considerable friction with some police officers, and this is not an uncommon washout stage for future Trial Assistants. But experienced Felony Trial Assistants are also assigned to the Unit for two-month stints, and there are plans to soon increase their number markedly.

Both in court and the police station, experienced prosecutors know the police personally, especially the Homicide-Sex and Robbery detectives. There is a good deal of trust that exists between them, though some distance is unavoidable and desirable. I have been called in to assist an investigation or interview a suspect because the detectives had simply reached a dead end and needed a fresh perspective from someone unfamiliar with the case. I've been talked out of rejecting charges on cases that led to convictions, and on occasion have had to refuse charges until the detectives look for more evidence, e.g. search again for the murder weapon, or check out an accused's alibi. I've been accidentally locked in interview rooms with murder suspects, have been left to guard an accused armed robber while the rest of the district frantically searches for the accomplice who had jumped out of a station window, and have split my pants while climbing a railroad embankment looking for a murder weapon, forcing me to take the subsequent court reported statement with my legs crossed.

Prosecutors and cops do stupid and inconsiderate

things and each can thereby infuriate the other, but being on the same side, products of the same system, and having spent vast amounts of time together, those who survive the winnowing process are true colleagues with enormous mutual respect and cooperation. *HSB* could enhance its realism, create tension and novel plot situations by integrating prosecutors into the show on a regular basis, perhaps as a continuing character(s) who operates both in the station and the courtroom. Such a role should recognize that prosecutors while in the field don't all wear three-piece suits. They often arrive at the station in down jackets and cords, carrying their folders, log book and beeper, driving their county radio car (unarmed, of course). These lawyers are as tough in the courtroom as the police are in the street (though routine street patrol work is more remote from the DA unless he is an ex-policeman as many are), and they are fully aware of the crime problem and the complications the courts create for police work.

I realize that this letter has been lengthy, but believe me when I say that I have abridged my thoughts considerably. Before I close it might be useful to tell you a bit about my background. I am 29 and grew up in Calumet City, Illinois, a tough blue-collar south suburb of Chicago bordering Hammond, Indiana. I was a philosophy major at Northwestern University and while at Harvard Law School, I clerked for the Suffolk County and Middlesex County District Attorneys' Offices. I have been an Assistant State's Attorney for over three years, and prior to becoming a State's Attorney, I clerked for two summers with the office in the felony trial courts. Currently I am assigned as a felony trial assistant to the criminal court building at 26th and California in Chicago. I have published several articles in political and legal philosophy, and coedited a book on criminal justice called *Assessing the Criminal*. I do not suggest that my background is typical, but significantly though my activities (and politics) may differ from the police with whom I work and from my fellow prosecutors, I have emerged from the same system, sharing many of the same instincts and attitudes as well as a healthy respect and genuine regard for most police officers.

Someday a successful show will recreate the genre of TV lawyer, both defense and prosecution, and it will probably be an MTM production. Until then there is room for the beginning of this development (and a future spin-off) in the *Hill Street Blues*. I think *HSB* has great potential and I wish you good luck in both the production and rating games. I hope this letter has been helpful in some way. Please feel free to contact me if you need any other information or assistance.

Sincerely,
Randy Barnett
Assistant State's Attorney
cc: Grant Tinker

In my cover letter to Grant Tinker, I offered this: "Although it primarily concerns 'Hill Street Blues,' it raises a number of possibilities for future MTM projects that I thought would be of particular interest to you." The first response I received was from Tinker himself, and it was unexpectedly flattering:

February 11, 1981

Mr. Randy Barnett
Assistant State's Attorney
Office of the State's Attorney
Cook County, Illinois 60608

Dear Mr. Barnett:

Thank you for your highly interesting letter of February 5; *it is far and away the most thoughtful reaction to one of our television programs that I can remember*

> *receiving* [emphasis added proudly]. I'm delighted that you addressed the original to Messrs. Bochco and Kozoll, since they are entirely responsible for HILL STREET BLUES. Like you, I'm largely pleased with the fruits of their efforts. Unlike you, I don't bring to my assessment of the show any particular expertise and therefore I don't find it lacking in any one area. Given your own background, and the points that you make in your letter, I'm persuaded that your judgements are valid. I'm sure that Michael and Steven will find them useful, as no doubt you'll hear from them.
>
> As a gratuitous added item, it may be that shows which are too authentic and "real," as opposed to glossy and fictional, don't make it with the audience as a general rule. LOU GRANT may be an exception. The fate of HILL STREET BLUES is still very much in the balance; to this point (seven shows aired), we are just lying there according to Nielsen. If the audience never finds us, or more correctly if we never find our audience, then we'll have to review the experience to get a sense of where we went wrong. The jury will probably stay out for another three or four weeks, at least.
>
> Thanks again for your reasoned and reasonable comments. I could probably arrange for you to have Gary Deeb's job if you wanted it.
>
> Best,
> Grant Tinker

His letter floored me. And I got a good laugh at his comment about Gary Deeb, the legendary syndicated TV columnist who then worked for the *Chicago Tribune*.

Of course, we now know that *Hill Street Blues* went on to be a monster hit; indeed, a cultural phenomenon. Steven Bochco's reply was somewhat less effusive: "Many thanks for your most interesting and informative letter. Your almost encyclopedic knowledge of television programming is quite unique, and it's always rewarding to know there

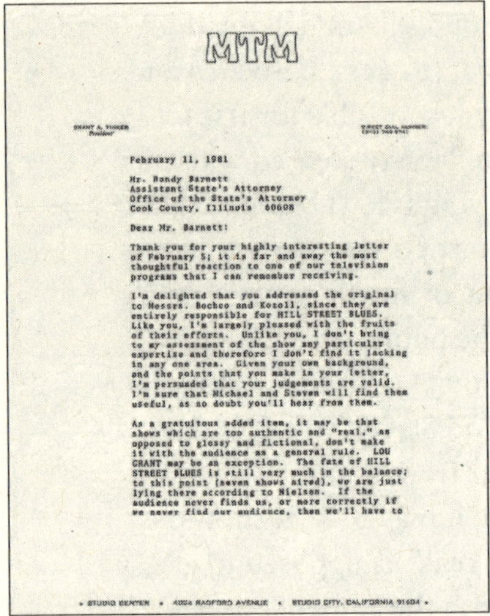

MTM

February 11, 1981

Mr. Randy Barnett
Assistant State's Attorney
Office of the State's Attorney
Cook County, Illinois 60608

Dear Mr. Barnett:

Thank you for your highly interesting letter of February 5; it is far and away the most thoughtful reaction to one of our television programs that I can remember receiving.

I'm delighted that you addressed the original to Messrs. Bochco and Kozoll, since they are entirely responsible for HILL STREET BLUES. Like you, I'm largely pleased with the fruits of their efforts. Unlike you, I don't bring to my assessment of the show any particular expertise and therefore I don't find it lacking in any one area. Given your own background, and the points that you make in your letter, I'm persuaded that your judgements are valid. I'm sure that Michael and Steven will find them useful, as no doubt you'll hear from them.

As a gratuitous added item, it may be that shows which are too authentic and "real," as opposed to glossy and fictional, don't make it with the audience as a general rule. LOU GRANT may be an exception. The fate of HILL STREET BLUES is still very much in the balance; to this point (seven shows aired), we are just lying there according to Nielsen. If the audience never finds us, or more correctly if we never find our audience, then we'll have to

• STUDIO CENTER • 4024 RADFORD AVENUE • STUDIO CITY, CALIFORNIA 91604 •

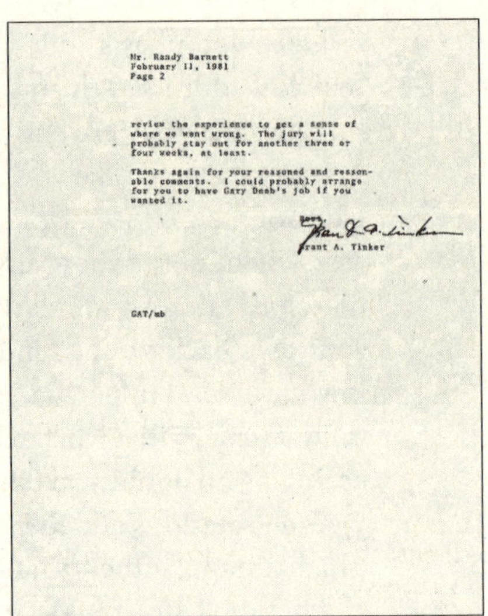

Mr. Randy Barnett
February 11, 1981
Page 2

review the experience to get a sense of where we went wrong. The jury will probably stay out for another three or four weeks, at least.

Thanks again for your reasoned and reasonable comments. I could probably arrange for you to have Gary Deeb's job if you wanted it.

Best,

Grant A. Tinker

GAT/mb

Figures 59-60. Letter from Grant Tinker

are individuals who care enough about what we do to share their expertise with us about what they do. In the future, we'll certainly attempt to give as much dimension and reality to police dealings with the legal profession as is possible within the dramatic framework of our series."

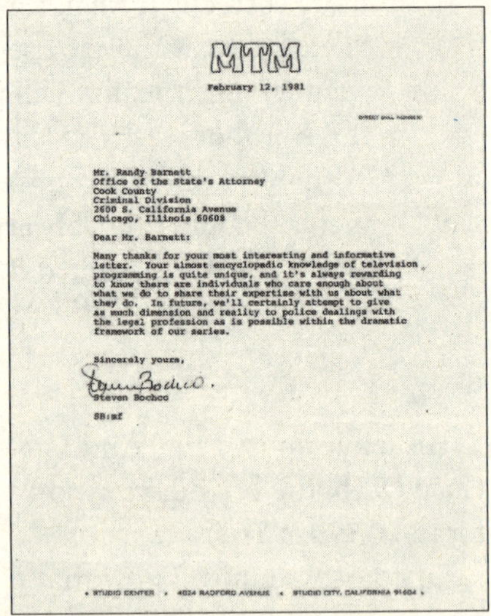

MTM

February 12, 1981

Mr. Randy Barnett
Office of the State's Attorney
Cook County
Criminal Division
2600 S. California Avenue
Chicago, Illinois 60608

Dear Mr. Barnett:

Many thanks for your most interesting and informative letter. Your almost encyclopedic knowledge of television programming is quite unique, and it's always rewarding to know there are individuals who care enough about what we do to share their expertise with us about what they do. In future, we'll certainly attempt to give as much dimension and reality to police dealings with the legal profession as is possible within the dramatic framework of our series.

Sincerely yours,

Steven Bochco

SB:mf

• STUDIO CENTER • 4024 RADFORD AVENUE • STUDIO CITY, CALIFORNIA 91604 •

Figure 61. Letter from Steven Bochco

At the time, I took the reference to my "almost encyclopedic knowledge of television programming is quite unique" to reflect bemusement as much as a compliment.

When I described in my letter the television depiction of a prosecutor as "a well-meaning, somewhat bookish if not effete lawyer who, though knowledgeable about the law, is obviously naive about the plight of the poor cop," and predicted that "[w]hen he or she does make an appearance, . . . the new DA stereotype, possibly a bit mellowed out and more sympathetic, will be adhered to," I had a particular actor in my mind's eye: George Wyner.

Wyner was a successful TV character actor whom I recalled from his role as DA Linnick on an episode of *Kojak*. So I thought it was particularly funny that, when Bochco and Kozoll eventually cast the role of DA Irwin Bernstein for *Hill Street Blues*, they hired the very same actor I was describing! Wyner would portray DA Bernstein in fifty-seven episodes of *HSB*.

Figure 62. George Wyner visits with relative police officer Sergeant Cip Siete while in Elgin for a family wedding, 1980 *(courtesy of the Elgin Area Historical Society)*

Turns out my work was not yet complete.

On September 15, 1986, as I began my fourth year as a law professor at the Chicago-Kent College of Law, *L.A. Law*, another MTM Production co-created by Steven Bochco, premiered on NBC. It ultimately ran for eight seasons and 172 episodes. Two days after its premiere, I sent Bochco another unsolicited review—or what Hollywood people call "notes":

Figure 63. Left to right, George Wyner, Veronica Hamel, and Daniel J. Travanti in *Hill Street Blues* *(courtesy of Cinematic/Alamy)*

> Nearly six years ago I wrote to you concerning the depiction of lawyers on *Hill Street Blues*. I urged you to abandon the "TV Lawyer" stereotypes that I described and to provide a more realistic characterization of criminal prosecutors than had been the industry custom. I also tried to explain how a fictional treatment of the problems really facing practicing lawyers could be more entertaining than most lawyer melodramas aired to date.
>
> At that time *Hill Street Blues* had been on the air less than two months and its future was uncertain, but both you and Grant Tinker were kind enough to answer

my letter. Moreover, while the character of "Irwin" the prosecutor initially lived down to my expectations and predictions, eventually he was given a somewhat more accurate and sympathetic demeanor. (The irony is that when I described the stereotypical prosecutor in my letter to you, the actor I specifically had in mind was one who had depicted a prosecutor on *Kojak*—the very actor you hired to play Irwin!)

At the close of my letter, I predicted that someone would eventually produce a successful lawyer show equivalent to *Hill Street Blues* and it would probably be MTM. I was close. Judging by its premiere episode, your production of *L.A. Law* is the show I had in mind. You are to be commended for going beyond the sphere of criminal law to build a show that can explore virtually every aspect of legal practice, in the way *St. Elsewhere* can deal with all aspects of medical practice. Given the obvious restrictions of prime time television, *L.A. Law* captures much of what is dramatic and interesting about lawyers' work and, as you continue to develop the characters, the show will certainly get even better.

Still, *L.A. Law* suffers from one persistent and seemingly incurable television deficiency: the depiction of prosecutors. Television seems incapable of depicting a prosecutor as being anything but completely ineffectual in and out of court. Perhaps this is because without an ineffectual prosecutor "the system" cannot as easily be made to appear quite so treacherous.

In the premiere episode, while the defense attorney and female judge were combining to humiliate the rape victim-witness (at a preliminary hearing), the prosecutor made no real effort to come to her assistance. At the next hearing, the prosecutor had apparently not conferred with the complainant before putting her on the stand. At the conclusion of the guilty plea hearing, the prosecutor left the victim sitting alone in the courtroom. And I cannot resist pointing out that the "brilliant" maneuvering of "Victor Sifuentes" to free his client as the prosecutor mumbled helplessly was utterly ridiculous.

Now I realize that fiction is fiction and that your principal characters are defense attorneys. And I admit that you can readily find examples of incompetent and insensitive prosecutors in every office in the country. But there are three important problems with consistently depicting the legal system absent an effective prosecutor.

First, it is unfair to the many hardworking and excellent prosecutors in this country who care as much about crime victims as "Michael Kuzak." After all (unlike "Kuzak" who left the DA's office), they choose to prosecute criminals for a living (usually at rather low pay), rather than defend them. (In the same regard, Joyce Davenport's brief flirtation with the DA's office on *Hill Street* was quite insulting to prosecutors generally—as though the only way to be true to one's principles is to be a PD.)

Second, dramatically it detracts from the alleged "brilliance" of the central characters to be doing legal combat with a blotter or a boob. In contrast, I again cite to you the example of James Stewart's defense attorney character contesting with George C. Scott's Assistant Attorney General character in *Anatomy of a Murder*. What made Stewart's eventual victory truly triumphant, brilliant, and entertaining was the perception that his opposition was extraordinarily competent. Surely it was for dramatic purposes—not a desire to positively depict prosecutors—that the local, incompetent DA was pushed aside by Scott's character. While Scott's character is mainly provided as a foil for Stewart's character, and eventually is made to blunder badly, I urge you to take a look at this movie to see how Stewart's defense attorney–hero character and the movie as a whole greatly benefit from being provided with worthy opposition.

(An example of a prosecutor-hero character who is not a mere foil would be Vincent Bugliosi in *Helter Skelter*.)

Finally, and most importantly, this persistent depiction of prosecutors does a great disservice to crime victims. For without a competent and strong prosecutor at his or her side, the system would routinely chew up the victim. Citizens who are given the inaccurate impression that such practices represent the norm will be much less likely to submit themselves to legal proceedings. It would be as though malpractice was depicted as the norm at *St. Elsewhere*. Who would ever want to go to a hospital?

I realize that shows such as *Hill Street, St. Elsewhere,* and *L.A. Law* maintain their entertainment value by depicting the "underbelly" of the system, and that it is difficult to do this while showing instances of how the system sometimes "works." What could be more boring? (Yet "Kuzak" made the system "work" in this episode, didn't he?)

So how about this suggestion: why not bring on board as a semi-regular or regular, an actor or actress to accurately and sympathetically portray a prosecutor—to provide a prosecutor's "role-model" if you will, much as "Ann Kelsey" is supposed to represent well-intentioned (and women) lawyers; in short, why not have a regular to play a competent and sympathetic Hamilton Burger to Kuzak's and Sifuentes' Perry Mason? Every "private eye" show needs a regular character depicting a sympathetic and usually competent cop "on the inside of the system" to advance the storyline—for example, "Dennis Becker" on *Rockford*. Why not borrow this kind of device for a lawyer show?

This device will let the audience know that such persons exist and will provide a worthy foil to pit against Kuzak and Sifuentes, enabling you to heighten the drama of their in-court and out-of-court confrontations.

> While, of course, the action must still revolve around "McKenzie, Brackman & Chaney," when you feel like showing that the system can work you can have this prosecutor beat them. When you want the system to fail, you can show this character's "feet of clay" (as you will routinely do with all your characters), or you can just import the sort of helpless and ineffectual DA's as appeared on the premiere show. As you well know, showing the professional and personal weaknesses of regular characters (as has been done with most of the characters on *St. Elsewhere*) has far more dramatic impact than when "guest" actors are used for this purpose.
>
> Please do not take this letter the wrong way. As I wrote six years ago about *Hill Street Blues*, "to criticize the show for lack of realism is to compliment the effort. . . ." You have proven that you know how to make a "realistic" television show entertaining. I am just suggesting that *L.A. Law* can be made even more entertaining by the injection of a bit more "reality."
>
> Good luck in the ratings. Please feel free to contact me if I can be of any assistance.

* * *

Bochco's reply was both courteous and curt: "Dear Professor Barnett: Thanks for your letter regarding our portrayal of prosecutors. I'm not sure I agree with your assessment altogether, but nevertheless stay tuned. Our Van Owen character (I believe) fits your bill. Let us know."

Indeed, the character "Grace Van Owen," portrayed by actress Susan Dey, was a savvy and ambitious L.A. deputy district attorney. She reminded me of Alice Richmond, the Harvard-grad, Suffolk County DA for whom I interned—including the fact that both were attractive blondes. So, at last, we had a sympathetic portrayal of a prosecutor as competent, ethical, tough. But her character would eventually become a partner at the law firm "McKenzie, Brackman, Chaney, and Kuzak."

Thus ended my attempt to have prosecutors more realistically and sympathetically portrayed by Hollywood—that is, until I portrayed a prosecutor in *InAlienable*. When I came off the set of that movie between scenes, other actors would compliment me: "You really look like a prosecutor in there," said one.

Figure 64. "You really look like a prosecutor" *(courtesy Michelle Short)*

Eventually, shows like *Law & Order* and its various spin-offs presented prosecutors as competent champions of justice. Characters like "Jack McCoy" (Sam Waterston) are seen as tough, principled, and dedicated to ensuring the guilty are punished and the innocent are protected. Former *Star Trek: Next Generation* actor Marina Sirtis, who played the assistant attorney general in *InAlienable*, was a huge *Law & Order* fan.

But I never thought the *Law & Order* series captured the tone of the real-world criminal justice system, especially how people talk to each other. There was too much speechifying or lecturing. A more true-to-life tone was portrayed by *NYPD Blue* and *The Wire*—both cop shows, not lawyer shows. *NYPD Blue* was another Steven Bochco production, though I believe the edgier, more realistic dialogue was provided by his co-creator, David Milch, who went on to produce *Deadwood*. And my trial partner Irv Miller would become the technical advisor for *The Good Wife*. On two occasions, he steered the writers to me for my input about constitutional issues that arose on that show.

So now you know how being a real prosecutor was better than TV, though with the growth of uncensored, "premium" streaming series, there's no good reason why fiction cannot capture the zeitgeist of what being a big city prosecutor in a corrupt legal system is really like.

Maybe someday it will.

INDEX